INSPIRED FORGIVENESS

Hidden Secrets
by Karlene Rickard

Published by
Filament Publishing Ltd
14, Croydon Road,
Beddington,
Croydon, Surrey CR0 4PA

www.filamentpublishing.com
+(44) 20 8688 2598

ISBN 978-1-915465-96-2

Inspired Forgiveness by Karlene Rickard
© 2023 Karlene Rickard

The right to be reconised as the author of this work has been asserted by Karlene Rickard in accordance with the Copyright and Designs Act 1988

All rights reserved

Contents

Acknowledgments		9
Introduction		10
Chapters		
1.	In the Beginning	11
2.	Life in UK	13
3.	Marriage and motherhood	16
4.	Totally paralysed	22
5.	Recovery	24
6.	Fallen again	26
7.	Transition	37
8.	Born Again	41
9.	An unexpected relationship	45
10.	He speaks, why not sensitise your ears?	52
11.	The journey began	55
12.	Who can understand?	59
13.	Restoration	61
14.	The vision	63
15.	Hurricane Gilbert	66
16.	There is always better	74
17.	Found a friend	78

18.	What's for you, is yours	81
19.	Home coming	90
20.	The pain of separation	93
21.	Can it get better?	97
22.	Yet another miracle	102
23.	Standing alone	109
24.	God delivers again	114
25.	Not every goodbye is gone	120
26.	Not every shut eye ain't dead	124
27.	New beginning	128
28.	Ushered into purpose	141
29.	God has not given us fear	145
30.	Value in counselling	147
31.	For ever mysterious	152
32.	Another mystery	157
33.	Now I understand	169
34.	He cuts and heals	178
35.	A friend from England	185
36.	The next stage	191
37.	He is constant - the same today as yesterday	198
38.	The future	202

Acknowledgements

I could not have written this book on my own so I would like to thank the many people who supported me along this journey. I would like to begin by thanking God for placing the idea for writing the book, in my head and for creating new openings for me to get this book published, when other doors had been closed.

My life is blessed with loyal friends, some of whom were my additional pairs of eyes by reading and commenting on my writing, so for this I would like to thank Jacqueline Thompson, Ankhara Lloyd-Hunte, Chris Day and Ermine Benjamin.

And finally, my grand-daughter, Matylin and my grandson Shay whose love and affection kept me positive.

Introduction

Karlene Rickard is an educator, parenting specialist, counsellor, licensed reverend, and author. Her first publication being the Empowerment for Parents Parenting Programme. This was followed by a number of books using the 'A to Z' of model. Karlene has also written about her relationship with God.

In this latest book Karlene expands on her relationship with the Lord as she chronicles her childhood in Jamaica, meeting her mother and family for the first time in the UK, challenges in Education, marriage, motherhood, and parenting. Her life's journey has had its ups and downs, positives and negatives, challenges and triumphs. Through it all she has clung to her faith.

In writing this autobiography Karlene has had to go back and remember events, incidents, comments, and remarks made over the course of her life. This in itself results in reliving and revisiting trauma. Delving into hidden secrets not shared with anyone before. Dredging up painful memories, experiencing the pain and hurt and deciding what to do with it. Karlene has chosen forgiveness.

In this autobiography Karlene reflects on the power of forgiveness as an act of love which sets us free and gives us peace. To forgive a conscious decision is made to stop blaming, punishing or being angry with someone for something they have said or done to us. Not only do we need to use our mouth to say we forgive, but we have to use our heart. This ensures that all grudges and bitterness is extricated from within, and we can let go. We acknowledge the hurt and move on. By forgiving others we forgive ourselves.

Chapter 1

In the Beginning

As a young girl growing up in Jamaica with my grandmother, I had the most wonderful time shooting birds with catapult, playing marbles with the boys, riding on coconut bow the branch of a coconut tree, riding cows and doing a range of boyish activities. Washing, ironing, and cooking were not a part of my agenda, to me that was what young ladies did and that was not me. The beatings from my grandmother did not deter me, in fact it made me more defiant. What I enjoyed most was going to the bush, armed with my machete and hoe, with papa, my step granddad. He had who looked after and raised me from the time I was three months old.

I can recall a particular occasion when my mother sent me a beautiful blue dress from England. Most girls would have been thrilled but not me. My gran was more excited! Calling me by my pet name which I had inherited from my mother's maiden name, McCarthy, my gran said, 'Mackie, tomorrow, (Saturday) we will go to Christiana Town (our main shopping area) to buy ribbons, socks and a pair of shoes to wear with the dress on Sunday.' I did not want to hear that, so early that Saturday morning, before the cock crowed, I woke up, got dressed, and sneaked out of the yard with papa, clutched my machete, and went to the bush.

We settled on a rock, papa made a fire and put a small freshly dug yam to be roasted. The fresh morning air clothed my body and the fulfilling sounds of the early morning creatures searching in the bushes made me feel at home. As I was about to sup the spring water, from the cocoa leaf cup my papa had fashioned for me, we heard a commotion. It was my grandma rushing through the growth with a switch. I dropped the cocoa leaf cup of water wetting all over my dress. I pounced like a gazelle and turned toward my grandma passing her like a flash of lightning. She dressed back and I sped along the dirt path, bare footed, to the main road. The sheer stones were uncomfortable under my feet. I headed straight for home. Amazingly my grandma was not too far behind, as I sped through the shopping square. There was a cacophony of sounds laughter and the words 'beat her Miss Grace'. I just kept running I don't think Usain Bolt could have out run me. At last I was home. There was no time to take a breather. I poured a jug of water in the basin and washed.

My life was punctuated with many such episodes. I really should have disliked my grandma, but I knew even from a young age that she loved me and wanted the best for me. I reciprocated my love by constantly showering her with readings from the Bible. My grandma was not literate, but she loved the Bible and she loved to hear me reading it to her. I always read at night, as we lived near the main road and every time I heard passers-by I would increase my volume and use more expressions. I knew in the morning I would be the talk of the community, 'Mackie can read good', my grandmother was so proud of me she would strut about like a peacock.

All that changed when I joined my mother and new family in the UK. I was 12 years of age and this was the first time I would be seeing my mother since she left me, in Jamaica, aged 3 months old.

Chapter 2

Life in the UK

The new life did not meet my expectations. I missed my old life.
My grandmother travelled with me. We landed in Manchester. It was winter and it was cold inside and cold outside. It was also damp. I wanted to return home to Jamaica so did my grandma. My mother had to book a return flight for grandma but she made it quite clear that I was not going anywhere but Wolverhampton. For the short period my grand stayed it was bearable but when she left I was devastated.

I was born on the same date and month as my mother and apparently we looked alike, this resemblance was totally confirmed after her death. Growing up I did not know and had not met many of my mother's friends. Mother had kept me as a secret in her life. When the myriad of my mother's friends arrived at her wake and I opened the doors to numerous individuals they all echoed the same thing 'You don't need any introduction.'

I was not pleased with my mother, I felt she resented me, but it was two sided. I did not want to be there and be in that family so I made very little effort to integrate. My parents appeared to favour my siblings. Eventually I tried just being a good daughter and in the process I bonded with my stepfather. I was the son he always wanted. We had a lot in common, and were for ever discussing cricket, gardening, wall papering and in his latter years, wine making. Later I bonded with my immediate sister. She was just over a year younger than me. Together we became the carers for our baby sister. She helped me live life like a girl and we became good friends. This friendship enabled me to overlook my mother's attitude towards me. In time I settled in the new community and my new school. They had placed me in the special needs class despite the fact I was an accomplished student arriving in the country with a good common entrance grade. This was equivalent to the eleven plus. My mother had not taken interest in my education. My sister accompanied me to the school. She was attending. I should have registered at Wolverhampton Grammar school. The UK and Jamaica, through the common wealth treaty, had a special relationship. This meant it was my right to attend the grammar school. The UK system recognised my qualification as a bonified grammar school student. I forgave my mother.

School became fun. I accepted that I would not make it in medicine due to the fact that, aged 12, I had been placed in a special needs class. This was one of my first major mistakes in my life. I accepted defeat by not aiming for my goal to become a paediatrician.

I tried very hard to be at peace with my mother, after all she was my mother. I loved her and was proud to have a mother with such a notable profession; sister in charge of midwifery at the hospital in Wolverhampton. The relationship improved but could not be compared with the relationship I had with my sisters. Perhaps I defeated myself by not aiming for my goal. My mother got on so well with sister, who wanted to be a teacher. My mother, was once a teacher, so in my immature logic I said, 'If I became a teacher my mother would care more for me.'

At the end of my final summer term in school with a few exam passes, when students were deciding on the next stage of life, there was an opportunity to select a teachers' college from those with vacancies. Given medicine was my initial career desire I should have followed my mother's footsteps and gone into nursing. Instead I applied to a teachers' training college. Bretton Hall in Yorkshire, it was miles away from home. I applied not expecting anything positive to happen. Amazingly I was called for an interview.

It was a beautiful place set in acres of land. The drive in from the main road had a canopy of tall arching oak trees which transitioned in to colourful rhododendrons on both sides of the driveway. On the left side I could see an artisan fountain and at the end of the drive way there was a plateau with a magnificent building. To the right of that in the distance were some small modern buildings and behind them was an amphitheatre. Below that was a lake. The site was breath taking. The air was fresh and pure which was evident as the trees were mostly oak, which will only grow in a pollution free atmosphere.

The interview went well, they loved me and I loved them, it seemed like a fait accompli, but later I realised why. I was one of only three black female students in the college. The other two bucked the trend as they had status and wealth. One came from Grenada and the other had a role in a regular TV series. It was a tremendous three years that shaped my life. My knowledge and experience of community work impacted the lives of many of my fellow students and our lecturers. Although I was a secondary trainee I volunteered to teach in the local primary where many of the lecturers' children attended. I insisted that all parents who had children in my class had to attend my meetings. Years letter in the county hall, in London, one of the lecturers recognised me. He told me that he and his wife were able to work with ethnic minorities in London because of my impact both in the college and in the primary school.

After my teaching practice I was offered a teaching position I still was not sure if I was that good and after three winters in Yorkshire, I could not afford another, Yorkshire is so cold and coldness and I are not friends, even in the Summer term I wear my coat and scarf, sometimes my gloves.

Chapter 3

Motherhood

I became pregnant because of abuse. I was so angry when I found out, my immediate reaction was to have an abortion. I constantly asked how this could have happened. I was an icon in the community well respected, being steeped in community activities. I now had a close relationship with my parents. I was also getting proposals from many suitors irrespective of ethnicity. I was very proud of my standing and my accomplishments. How could I live with this? I went to my local clinic and discussed my situation with a medical practitioner. Several options were put forward. I decided abortion was the only way out and I completed the relevant forms. I was given a document to attend a clinic in Coventry. That suited me as my sister was living there. I phoned her under the pretext that I would be coming to spend some time with her. She was oblivious of my condition. Whilst there, the would-be father visited and we spent time together.

We were now engaged.

I am not sure he loved me, but he wanted to prove to all those who were clamouring after me that I belonged to him. I certainly did not love him, but I held him in high esteem. His knowledge of Back history was incredible. He was bold and confident. I loved his vision to empower black youth, especially boys, and to give black people a voice. I wanted to be a part of that journey. He too, was unaware of my condition. As I reflected and listened to my inner voice, I was convicted and convinced, even though I was not yet a born-again Christian, not to abort my innocent child. I guess God was talking to me. Before long I revealed my secret to my sister. I telephoned the father and requested that we get married immediately, which he consented to. Why I really don't know. Within a short period we arranged a civil wedding in London. I invited my mother, but she was not interested, so the ceremony was attended by just two witnesses - my sister and the groom-to-be's best friend. Afterwards, the four of us dined in a lovely restaurant followed by a small reception with his friends in another restaurant in Brixton.

I resigned from my position as head of biology in a comprehensive school in Wolverhampton and moved to live with my new husband in a small one bedroom first-floor council flat in London. We got on very well when we were together, but those moments were not often, as he made good use of my car visiting ladies. Whilst he was out, I had lots of threatening calls from various women. One woman had the audacity of calling and stated that I was falsely accusing him of being the father of my child and I needed to leave his flat with his car and find the real father of my child. Every day I got angrier, but when I reflected on the damage I could cause to the unborn foetus, I relaxed, released him from heart and embraced my pregnancy.

One night whilst I sat alone, I cried. I was past the due date by nearly a month. The pregnancy was cumbersome and I felt trapped. Full of anger and hatred I cried out to God for help. As I released all the negative emotions there was a settled peace so I decided to have a warm bath. It was relaxing. I guess I must have been asleep because I was startled by the closing of the front door and soon became aware that my pregnancy water had broken. The bath was cool. He called out to me, as I was not in the bedroom. I answered. He came and stood at the doorway. Riddled with pain I told him what had happened. He carefully took me from the bath, tenderly dried my body, dressed me, placed me on the back seat of the car and drove at lightning speed to the hospital. On arrival I was taken into the delivery room. There were two doctors attending to me. The birth was a difficult one. I was overdue, my waters had broken, and the head of the baby was not properly positioned for delivery. A student doctor was holding my hand and my husband was taking pictures with my camera. I was annoyed as I needed my husband to be comforting me not a stranger. Eventually it was over. They had to cut me in order for the head to come out freely. We were rushed out of the labour suite – my baby was sent to the special care baby unit and I was sent to the maternity ward. I remember asking the nurse if my son was okay, she said 'Yes but both of you are critical,' then she added "Don't worry about feeding him, he will be in the incubator. Just rest we will look after both of you". As I lay in the bed, I thought about the experience, and the fact that more than likely he was chasing after women in my car. I felt angry and I wanted to kill him. Overcome with regrets, my thoughts focused on how I had ruined my life. I cried out earnestly again to God and immediately I sensed His presence. It felt safe, and comfortable so I repented, there was such a wonderful peace, so I decided once again to let go, forgive, and sleep. I do not know how many hours or days that I slept for. When I woke from my slumber, I asked for some tea, the lady opposite my bed spoke, ""How do you do it?", "Do what?" I retorted. She responded 'Every time your child needed feeding you woke up, walked to the nursery with your eyes closed, fed him and returned to your bed. He was not given one bottle by the attending nurse.' I just turned over and went to bed as it made no sense. When I woke up the nurse confirmed what the lady had said. The practise continued and the other four mothers on the ward who were white became hostile. They all had a normal birth and yet none of their children took to being breast-fed. I desperately wanted to leave but I had a serious tear which meant I had to stay. At last, my husband was summoned to collect me. I requested a particular dress and shoes, but he turned up empty handed! Again, I was furious at having to leave the hospital in my dressing gown and slippers. He was so excited about his son that en route home he made lots of stops, each time taking out the tiny baby all around Camden to show friends. I was tired and frustrated but kept my peace. What should have been twenty minutes' journey took over an hour, when we eventually arrived safely home. I placed our son in a basket I had padded and prepared for him. I fed and cared him.

After three months I started to have itchy feet. I wanted to take my baby son out to see friends and most of all my parents. He was incredibly beautiful. One morning I woke up and got both of us ready. To be honest, I did not know the whereabouts of my husband, but my car was there, parked outside. I packed and carefully went down the stairs firstly with our clothes then with my son, who was fast asleep in the basket. I placed him safely on the back seat and got in the driver's seat. I knew it was a risk, but I wanted my son to meet his grandparents. A thought came before me – the journey ahead was over a hundred miles, most of it motorway - but that did not deter me. I set off to Wolverhampton, driving carefully and after several hours I pulled up, exhausted, in my parents' driveway. I rang the bell and my mother answered and opened the door. She was shocked, but excited, as I had not phoned ahead of time. She was excited to see her grandson. The first grandchild. My mother was a senior midwife and she had three girls, so we were in safe hands. Nevertheless, I was shocked by her excitement as in the past she made it known that she did not like boys. I was profoundly grateful to God and I forgave my mother totally for the journey I had made with her, since arriving in the UK. After a wonderful time, I made the journey back to London and on arrival, instead of going to God and immediately I sensed His presence. It felt safe, and comfortable so I repented, there was such a wonderful peace, so I decided once again to let go, forgive, and sleep. I do not know how many hours or days that I slept for. When I woke from my slumber, I asked for some tea, the lady opposite my bed spoke, "'How do you do it?', "Do what?" I retorted. She responded 'Every time your child needed feeding you woke up, walked to the nursery with your eyes closed, fed him and returned to your bed. He was not given one bottle by the attending nurse.' I just turned over and went to bed as it made no sense. When I woke up the nurse confirmed what the lady had said. The practise continued and the other four mothers on the ward who were white became hostile. They all had a normal birth and yet none of their children took to being breast-fed. I desperately wanted to leave but I had a serious tear which meant I had to stay. At last, my husband was summoned to collect me. I requested a particular dress and shoes, but he turned up empty handed! Again, I was furious at having to leave the hospital in my dressing gown and slippers. He was so excited about his son that en route home he made lots of stops, each time taking out the tiny baby all around Camden to show friends. I was tired and frustrated but kept my peace. What should have been twenty minutes' journey took over an hour, when we eventually arrived safely home. I placed our son in a basket I had padded and prepared for him. I fed and cared him.

After three months I started to have itchy feet. I wanted to take my baby son out to see friends and most of all my parents. He was incredibly beautiful. One morning I woke up and got both of us ready. To be honest, I did not know the whereabouts of my husband, but my car was there, parked outside. I packed and carefully went down the stairs firstly with our clothes then with my son, who was fast asleep in the basket. I placed him safely on the back seat and got in the driver's seat. I knew it was a risk, but I wanted my son to meet his grandparents. A thought came before me – the journey ahead was over a hundred miles, most of it motorway - but that did not deter me. I set off to Wolverhampton, driving carefully and after several hours I pulled up, exhausted, in my parents' driveway. I rang the bell and my mother answered and opened the door. She was shocked, but excited, as I had not phoned ahead of time. She was excited to see her grandson. The first grandchild. My mother was a senior midwife and she had three girls, so we were in safe hands. Nevertheless, I was shocked by her excitement as in the past she made it known that she did not like boys. I was profoundly grateful to God and I forgave my mother totally for the journey I had made with her, since arriving in the UK. After a wonderful time, I made the journey back to London and on arrival, instead of going directly back to our home I went to a mutual friend. It was exhausting walking up three flights of winding stairs. She was on the top floor. I sat around her table, placed the basket on the table and rested for a while. I then went down the steps back to the car leaving my son with our friend. I went to our one bedroom flat alone. The flat was tastefully decorated. As I entered the small living room my husband was sitting on our wicker chair and a Caucasian young lady was swinging in our hummock. Needless to say I was furious but kept my peace. I turned around and left the flat and drove back to our friend's home. Furious I flew up the stairs burst into the room and flopped on the chair putting my full handbag on the table; I had collected lots of nick and knacks, including my dissecting kit from my parents' home. Pianki was no longer on the table as my friend had put the basket safely on her bed. I gasped for breath and told our friend what I had seen in my flat. With elbows on the table I cushioned my face in my open hands forcing back the tears. My husband must have chased after me on foot judging by what happened within ten minutes of me talking with my friend. Her ten-year-old daughter was looking out of the window. She knew my husband, whom she called uncle. Once she sighted him, she rushed down and opened the door and let him in. With his long legs he must have climbed two or even three steps at a time. Unexpectedly this angry frame filled the doorway. He walked over to me and struck me across the head propelling me into the air. I fell on the table breaking it into two and ended up lying on the pieces alongside the contents of my handbag. He kept kicking me, one foot after another, in my tender stomach having given birth only three months earlier. He then stopped. I struggled to my feet grasping a scalpel. I guess it had fallen from the dissecting kit, out of my handbag, among the things I had collected from my parents' home. I don't know how it got into my hand, but it gave me the confidence to fight back. I stood up on wobbly legs with vengeance in my eyes, he too started to shake slowly backing away to the kitchen counter, as I moved closer towards him. The kitchen counter blocked his attempt to exit. I saw fear in his eyes. My friend came along side me and held my hand. I heard when she said 'You don't want to go prison for him', at the same time as taking the scalpel out of my hand.

    I don't know what happened next but I woke up with a bright light that seemed strange. Even with the electric light on the room was not bright, the flat was dull so I really thought I had died and arrived in heaven. I was disappointed when I discovered I was in the theatre of the same hospital where I had given birth. After the doctor examined me I was put into a private room with a policeman on guard at the door. One day I just lying there in bed when I heard the booming voice of my husband. I turned to look at the door and there he was, bigger and taller than my police guard. He was not allowed to enter my room. I called my guard and asked him to permit my husband to enter for moment. He came in looking almost remorseful I looked at him and asked 'Why?' His response was 'I don't know'. I shouted 'Officer please remove this man!'

I was in the hospital for a few days and our son was with my friend. During that period women that I had never met before, came with affidavits asking me to put him away so he would not hurt any more women, I was devastated but took no notice of their requests. Once I was discharged, I engaged a solicitor and filed for divorce. I went to live with my auntie. She helped me to secure a council maisonette in the borough of Hackney in London and my husband was charged by the court not to be found within a given distance of where I lived. Shortly afterwards I was summoned to appear at the Strand. There we came face to face, for the first time after the attack. In the court room we started to argue because neither of us had a lawyer. The judge sent us out of the courtroom to resolve our differences We did but he threatened that he would be after me if I took his son to church. We went back into the courtroom where I was granted a divorce. I became a single mother and received support from family and friends. There were lots of challenges included being totally paralysed, when Pianki (Mark) was six years old, and returning Jamaica to live with the pastor of a small independent fellowship. We endearingly called the pastor of the Church of God church, Mom K. She supported us, which enable my son to go to a good prep school. We spent a lot of fun moments together, but he was always in a lot trouble. In Jamaica 'beating' was their way of disciplining children. Needless to say he had more than his fair share but that did not affect his intellectual development. He left prep school with a study Bible for being an accomplished student. He attended Glenmuir High one of the top co-educational schools in Jamaica. He received an excellent letter of recommendation which afforded him a place into a good high school in UK. This was followed by studying at two universities, and a prestigious teacher training college. He is now a successful teacher married with his own children.

Chapter 4

Totally Paralysed

One sunny day in June 1983 I was driving with my son, who was a year old, around Gower Street in central London. It was a lovely day. The searing heat reached my very core. It felt like Jamaica, just the medicine I needed. As we cruised along the mews looking at some lovely blossoming trees, in a small park embroidered by the classical buildings of London university, located across the road from Euston Station, one of the main tube and train stations, I mused myself with the unrecognised joyful chatter of my energetic bright boy. He was clearly fascinated by his environment, he kept pointing at passers-by and the lovely buildings, my heart rejoiced.

Suddenly things changed. My right leg felt uncomfortable, in fact spasmic. Luckily, we were five minutes from one of the large hospitals in London, University College Hospital. I drove cautiously to the hospital. On arrival there was one parking place in front of casualty. I skilfully manoeuvred into the space which was quite an achievement as I'd always found reversing and parking challenging. The car was safely parked in an ideal spot in front of the entrance to the hospital. Not too far to walk. Any further away I would not have made it, as the heaviness in my legs was pronounced. I had sat in the car for a few moments and prayed for help to come along side. Pianki could not wait to get out he was like a Jack-in-the-box

Casualty was throned with weary looking faces. It was hot, but my son was so excited just bouncing up and down, he brought smiles to some faces as they looked on. I wanted to go back to the car, but just then I spotted a seat and managed to get there before anyone else. I sighed and sat down with relief. My son was oblivious to my condition, but what could I have expected from a one-year-old. His audience was amused which added fuel to his antics! My son had brought joy to some of the faces.

I had not long sat down when both my legs started to stiffen and stick out causing my position on the chair to change. I felt like a slat of board lent across the back and front of the chair. There was a gap between me and chair. Fear gripped me, and I cried "Nurse!" Two came running and without communicating to me, one shouted to a porter to bring a wheelchair. Many of the weary faces looked towards me. I guess it was a wonderful way to be attended to first, but putting fun aside, I was afraid. Not even conscious of what was happening to my son, I must have passed on the relevant information as my auntie in Hackney had collected him. My mind was overloaded and empty at the same time, how is that possible. Certainly this is an oxymoron. I was transferred on to a bed, the nurse carried out various tests then the doctor passed by and he immediately admitted me. My new residence was a spacious private room. I lay in the bed, which was designed for my body, reflecting on my life's journey. The things I valued the camera equipment, car, career and having fun paled into the back ground. I forced back the tears whilst muttering 'I have lost the freedom to move, how will I care for my son'. I stayed in the hospital for four months. In the first week I cried every day trying to make sense of what had happened. It was incredible one minute upright, in good health and in the blink of an eye I was lying down almost lifeless. My constant thought was, 'what is man that God is mindful of him. Who can really know the fate of man but God.'

Chapter 5

Recovery

After about a month of physiotherapy I was allowed to return home to live with my parents in Wolverhampton. My care was transferred to the local hospital. Pianki was collected from my auntie. My parents diligently cared for both of us. Thanks to me they had two children again to care for at a time when they should have been enjoying their freedom. I have to say that parenting is a lifetime commitment. It was my Dad's responsibility to take me almost daily to the physiotherapist and to other clinics. With care, love and the blessings of God I continued to make great progress. I was very eager to be responsible and independent again.

My recovery was phenomenal. It was within a matter of weeks that I was able to move about independently without being contorted, doing many of my former activities although a little uncoordinated and having problems with finer movements such as writing properly. Soon I went back in-part to my old lifestyle, meeting friends, going driving, and being involved in community activities. I felt a sense of independence. As I reflected on my life, pride started to worm its way through my thoughts. I considered myself to be an excellent science teacher with a deep love for the children. Furthermore, my dedication went beyond the class room and I worked within the children's community. I was highly motivated, self-determined and open to experience the things of God. I felt ready to start living again.

I left from under the protective wings of my family in Wolverhampton and returned to London with Pianki. I went into full-time employment as a community worker for Caribbean House, an African-Caribbean organisation which provided social, spiritual, educational and financial support for adults and young people of Caribbean descent. I was responsible for developing an education programme for teenagers who were excluded from mainstream schools because of their uncontrollable behaviour. They had all committed criminal offences (some more serious than others) but were too young to be locked away. They earned the grand title of being called 'recidivist', which means being a guest of Her Majesty's Service.

I was happy to be active in the community again albeit with physical and mental limitations. I was grateful to God that I was still able to do things independently again. I have always loved community work. As a child with my granddad in Jamaica, in England with dad into my teenage years and later as a trainee teacher in Yorkshire. The experience was different in that I was the only black person. My community involvement continued when I became a professional teacher in Wolverhampton. The work gave me a real sense of being and purpose.

The teaching post was challenging. The children and their parents were demanding. I was effective and got results but they wanted more. I gave a hundred and ten percent at the expense of spending quality time with Pianki. At the end of each day I was often mentally and emotionally exhausted. Nevertheless, I was driven by a need to be needed by the outside world. Sometimes as a single parent with a young child and working with children, I felt devoid of adult companionship. Eventually I started to crave adult company. Unexpectedly I was drawn to a rather vivacious, overpowering woman about my age, whose personality was similar to that of my ex-husband. They both liked to organise people's lives and I happened to be their subject. I needed to be cared for so I allowed her to organise my social and domestic life, even provision of a baby sitter (her brother) for Pianki.

Pianki and I became members of her family and I became a part of her social circle of four dynamic young women. They lived an extremely active social life - parties, theatre, and live music on Sundays by the river. At times they flirted with the occult, reading the tarot cards. Church for me was an occasional visit. I tried to immerse myself into lots of their activities with the exception of the occult, even though I watched as they played with the Tarot cards. I must admit that at times I was a little out of my depth. I was not feeling confident enough to be involved especially in their discussions and dances. But I was determined to be apart of the group and they were very protective of me.

Chapter 6

Fallen again

On a particular Sunday when everyone else could be found in the comfort of their homes or at church with their family I had taken on the responsibility to represent the organisation at a Chinese event. It was being held about ten minutes from the centre. I had asked others to help but they were not interested so I asked them to put together some of their work which I would collect and exhibit.

I was struggling with posters tucked under my chin and filling my arms, on that quiet Sunday morning, when I should have been in church. I could hardly see the path. I had under-estimated the distance and decided not to drive but it was quite far with the load. Alone, playing Miss Superwoman! I tried to feel my way along the path; one foot before the other. Under the weight of the papers I persevered. I knew it was too heavy but was determined not to make two or three trips. I had done half of the journey when my legs weakened and there was a cracking sound in my lower spine. I heard the sound. Then there was just pain, pain, and more intense pain. I related the pain to an experience when I was pregnant; "sciatica" (trapping of a main nerve along my groin) was the diagnosis. I concluded that I was experiencing sciatica again, just a temporary, pain.

I continued to struggle to the venue with my load. When I reached I was pleased to see my co-worker, a minister of the gospel, (at least he was not at church either). He decided to come and help me to set up the exhibition. His presence was like a breath of fresh air. By now the pain had intensified like an extremely bad nagging tooth-ache. It was obvious to him that I was in pain and he insisted that I should go to the hospital. I asked

At work I explored innovative ways to motivate and maintain the interest of the young people. Photography became my primary medium of teaching them reading and mathematics. The young people were motivated by the practical activities. They learned some essential mathematical principles and we developed a positive relationship. The project became a success. Relationship with their parents, adults, teachers and other young people both in their schools and outside improved. Several of the children were able to return to school. One father became a voluntary worker for the project. The success made me popular with the families, the Founder and other members of staff. It gave me a buzz. I started to meet the Founder regularly to discuss new ideas. He endorsed and supported every idea I put forward.

Over a very short period the organisation expanded to include training courses for social services, a publications department, a day-time club for the elderly, a meat shop and a drop-in centre. We were well funded by various funding bodies. The organisation purchased a hotel in Barbados for the elderly, clients and the workers; this was to provide both therapy and a break for families and staff. Great! After three years with the organisation, I had the opportunity to stay in the hotel with Pianki. All we had to provide was our fare.

Pianki and I spent five wonderful weeks in sunny Barbados. The hotel was located opposite the beach in the heart of the tourist industry, St. James. It had a swimming pool in the back and an excellent restaurant next door that catered for local taste. The sun, food, friendship and romance were all mine. I felt I had it made. I wanted it to last for ever. But it ended. I returned to England invigorated and ready to move mountains. Within me there was a zest for life, urgency and boundless energy for success. I worked harder than before, bemoaning the lack of hours in the day. My time of communication with God faded into the background.

him to accompany me to University College hospital where I was admitted before. It was not the nearest, but I knew it was one of the best hospitals in London, and I wanted to get the best treatment.

I had to drive, which was difficult. Before I reached the hospital, numbness started to creep up my legs. I was afraid, my stomach started to churn and I took rapid deep breaths, not wanting to believe the remotest possibility of becoming totally paralysed again. I parked and we went into casualty. It wasn't so busy. I reported to the nurse on duty, she took my details and I was admitted straight onto the investigation ward where patients are observed. I was shown to a bed and sat on it to wait for the consultant. My friend left. I felt alone as I waited. The wait seemed never ending. In the meantime, the numbness moved from my waist, to my toes. The right side felt more severe than the left side. I got very angry with the doctor. I wanted to scream. My mouth was dry and my palms sweaty. 'Where were they?' I muttered.

Eventually the consultant came, in fact the bed was surrounded by a team of medical experts and students, decked out in their white overcoats, with the exception of the consultant who wore a perfectly tailored suit. They had scarcely arrived before they bombarded me with questions; questions from every direction; prod, prod, prod here there and everywhere. It was as if musical notes were being played on my knees. They discussed me amongst themselves occasionally looking at me like an object. It was frustrating not knowing what was happening.

After what seemed to be a lifetime they were no wiser. They had no answer for me. It was then that the reality of being paralysed again struck home. The thought of having to stay in the hospital over-night made me weak and vulnerable. I looked directly into the eyes of the consultant and begged in earnest for an explanation, but he only looked at me. There was gentleness in his eyes. They all seemed mystified. The young students even seemed worried for me. I was afraid. Not again, I thought. I felt hopeless. The consultant placed his hand gently on my shoulder. It was a touch of assurance that they were going to do their best for me. The team moved on to the next patient. I was alone.

Once again I took up residence in the hospital. I really did not expect to be in hospital again. After the experience of being totally paralysed, I started to feel different about my life and the people around me. The need to be successful in my career and to acquire the best things which money could buy became less important. In fact, that desire paled into insignificance. All I wanted was to be available for people who needed help. I wanted to help, help, and just help.

There I was in the hospital this time paralysed from my waist to my toes, needing to be cared for, but swarmed by nurses, patients and others who sought advice on a range of issues. The answers flowed like a cool stream pouring through my mouth. The thirsty recipients drank and drank. I observed as they left seemingly contented.

I was no longer perturbed by contentions and disagreements around me. It was always a pleasure to help others to resolve what I considered to be minor issues. My experience was akin to that of a conduit through which all the solutions were channelled, yet, in the midst I was enshrouded by masses of soft clouds that kept me safe and warm. I found that whenever anyone with deep emotional issues drew near, my newly developed spiritual and emotional antenna detected their feelings to an extent where both their feelings and exact experience were transferred to me. Often when I reflected this to them, they would confirm it in words, or burst into tears and embrace me. Peoples' pain seemed tangible and obvious. Even before they chose to disclose what they were experiencing, I knew. I felt like a magnet attracting hundreds of iron fillings, human iron fillings, which fought to get close to me.

There was a rather well groomed elderly lady in the bed opposite. Whenever I looked across at her she had a solemn expression. On occasions I smiled, but she never reciprocated. The nurses constantly complained about her attitude and behaviour. 'She is being unpleasant, arrogant and pernicious,' I overheard as they expressed their dread and discomfort about having to care for her. I was eager to help. I could see that the nurses were overworked and needed to feel appreciated by us, the patients. But I wondered about the lady opposite. Had anyone considered her inner feelings? My thought was, 'Perhaps she had as much disdain for the nurses. Could it be that they represented all she wanted to forget, who knows!!'

One day as I looked across to her bed she appeared to be fast asleep. I felt compelled to drive over in my newly acquired wheelchair. After all, I needed to put my driving skills to the test. The nurses had transferred me onto the wheelchair with its black leathery seat that was hemmed in by its shiny metal arms and I could smell the newness of the rubber surrounding the glistening spokes. I clutched onto the controls and slid my hands around them manoeuvring myself in a circular motion.

I brought the chair to a standstill facing the lady's bed, then gently drove to the head of her bed and parked. I guess she sensed my presence, because she stirred, craned her head and looked up at me. My heart missed a beat, not knowing what to expect. She smiled. I greeted her. She positioned herself onto her side to face me and I accommodated her by manoeuvring the chair. It felt like a much overdue visit. She asked my name. Her's I cannot recall. She wanted to know so much about me. She commented on my constant stream of visitors which flattered me. Her tone of voice quaked and sadness enveloped her face. Not having children of her own she had provided handsomely for her nieces and nephews. They had deserted her as soon as she became very ill. The niece she trusted to ensure that her affairs were in order had abused that trust and squandered her wealth. She had to be transferred from the private wing of the hospital because the necessary insurance policy was not in place to maintain the care she desired.

I don't know how long I spent with her that day, but from then on I became a regular visitor, her only visitor outside of the nurses and doctors. We became friends. She continued to share her life's journey with me. We laughed and joked as she entertained me with stories of her adventures. Her persona would change as she sat erect, with radiance in her eyes and clearly spoken words interspersed with gentle hand movements and discreet chuckles.

With time my friend's facial expressions softened, her eyes were perpetually bright, and there was an air of warmth which encompassed her presence as if begging every passer by to be engaged with her. That once aged and wrinkled skin seemed to have shed its outer coat and was now clothed with exquisitely architectured hair-lined wrinkles around her eyes and lips framing two burning red cheeks with a welcoming smile. She emitted an aura of beauty and sensuousness. It was so easy to imagine her swaying on the dance floor in a beautiful well fitted embroidered silk ball gown, as suitors and others looked on with admiration.

My new friend who had lost life's vigour and created a crust of hostility and bitterness to mask the hurt and rejection she had experienced from relatives and friends had found her inner beauty. She no longer buried herself under the bedding, but emerged each morning, flaunting the elegant night gowns which embellished her God-given physical beauty, long neck, delicate facial features and long silver hair which often rested on her erect shoulders. Her chest was thrust forward as a young model ready to venture the catwalk. All this was once hidden behind her sullen demeanour.

Even the nursing staff that were often frustrated by her abruptness and dismissive attitude started to gravitate towards her. Often they left her bedside amused by her remarks. Some would say, 'Isn't she pleasant? I cannot believe it is the same patient.'

We became closer and started to talk about the future. No longer waiting to die, but to live and enjoy life again. We had many areas of interests in common. She was an avid reader of science fiction and factual material and possessed a range of books which she kindly offered me, for collection, once she was discharged. Two weeks later I woke up early in the morning and turned my face to greet her, to be confronted by an empty well made bed. I wanted to know where she was, but feared the worse which prevented me from asking immediately.

I could no longer contain myself, 'Nurse' I whispered looking toward where my friend laid.

'She died peacefully in her sleep'.

I felt as if every organ within cried out and I wanted to scream 'Why!' I managed to hold back the tears, but I could not stop the involuntary churning inside of my stomach. I laid and looked at the space with disbelief. The day passed by as I listened to the bustling noise on the ward. Ever so often I glanced over to the space that was occupied by my friend. Her memory lived on in my mind.

One day during the quiet period when the patients were resting and the nurses were writing their reports, I sat propped up in my bed looking across to where my new friend once lived and reflecting on our short but fruitful time together. Two young ladies conservatively dressed in long skirts, jackets and head covered clutching what appeared to be Bibles and leaflets entered the ward. I was distracted by the noise of the double door closing behind them. I stared as they moved from patient to patient, each time depositing a leaflet. I felt quite excited when they got closer to the alcove which I shared with two other patients. They went to the lady on my left. Soon it would be my turn, but they passed my bed, gazing at me. I felt cheated. Just as they were approaching the next bed, I piped up, 'why have you not stopped.'

One of the young ladies still in her stride, turned her head, and said

'You have the Mark.'

'The Mark,' I echoed, sinking into the pile of pillows behind my back. The statement left me wondering what the "Mark" meant.

I watched as the young ladies approached the next patient. I felt annoyed. 'That should have been me,' I thought. As I stared at them I remembered my confirmation class, when I was preparing to become a member of the United Reformed Church in Wolverhampton. My sister and I went to the church manse for our weekly session where our minister, Rev Campbell, taught us certain fundamentals in becoming a Christian and member of the church. After the final session Rev. Campbell looked directly at me and said 'Karlene I have taken many people through these classes and I have not met anyone like you before, you have the Mark.' I gave a sheepish smile, feeling quite embarrassed, as was a common reaction in my teenage years when I thought someone was being endearing. I never thought to ask him what he meant and he did not offer an explanation. Now here was that statement again.

Eventually, the mystery statement became apparent. Whilst attending a Bible study it was made clear that after a person declared a personal encounter and experience with Jesus Christ, that person tends to attract people's attention not only through fundamental changes in their behaviour, attitude and life-style, but there seems to be an aura, a presence which glows as it envelopes them. Others start to perceive that the recipient is different, although they are not always able to define it.

On reflection that difference must have happened at an early age because I had always been singled out by many older members of the community as being very special. I was extremely popular. I loved being in the presence of the elderly, enjoying the stories they told of old, their gentle touch as they stretched my plaits, the kind words of encouragement and the sweet melodies they sang to God.

When as a mature woman I visited my granddad in 2001, he cried as he said, 'Sis Karlene I remembered when you rescued the goat from the cliff face when there was a serious landside; no one else could. When you came back leading the goat everyone was shocked. You were good to everyone. When you had to go to England and we took you to the airport, you gave Patrick all the money you had saved for the trip. I wanted to pick you up and run away.' As I listened to him and saw the sadness in his eyes my legs started to buckle and I went and sat on his little veranda, wishing

I too could recall those memories, I couldn't, the illness had affected my memory, but at least I understand 'the Mark'.

For weeks they carried out numerous tests. I was taken to different departments for tests, travelling underground through the hospital's carefully designed labyrinth of tunnels. I felt like a secret agent being interrogated for betraying my country. I met many specialists, some friendly, some kind and others quite stark. One day I had a severe dispute with the psychiatrist. He was sent to me as the last resort. The team of doctors decided that all the tests were negative so the illness was not physiological therefore it had to be mental. I refused to accept their conclusion and to be subjected to psychological assessment and treatment. The senior consultant arrived at my bedside with a very pleasant bedside manner, but I was not cooperative. In a calm manner he tried to persuade me to give him a chance but I remained firm. He must have visited me over three days, but I ignored him, and eventually he got the message.

Unfortunately, my failure to cooperate caused the hospital to decide that there was very little they could do for me. The white coat army visits became infrequent and the stops at my bedside were brief. Visits from my family were fewer because the distance made it difficult for them. With the exceptions of the pastor (who visited nearly every day with fresh laundry) and Jessica and Eric, my friends. Eric collected me some week-ends. It was a long drive to their warm and comfortable home. The breeze on my face was therapeutic and the fresh air, green fields and people moving around in the open space was liberating. I felt like I was released from prison. The home cuisine made a pleasant change from hospital food. I would curl up on the floor as Eric diligently exercised the muscles in my legs. Needless to say, I always found the journey back to the hospital torturous.

The matron informed me that they were looking for a place for me in the disabled and elderly unit as the bed that I occupied in the investigation ward was needed. Just the thought that they had given up on me caused me to shudder. The administrative and medical team were in the process of arranging a date to meet and finalise the arrangement. Once again I checked in on God. 'Help' I cried.

I was answered in an incredible way. Whilst working at Caribbean House in Hackney I had become friendly with a young lady which resulted in me being apart of her family. A lovely family, she had three sisters, two older and one younger. The day before the hospital staff had their meeting one of the older sisters, visited unexpectedly. She came with a purpose, wanting to know all about what was being arranged by the hospital. This was unusual because she was neither family nor a close friend. Anyway I shared what the hospital had decided to do. Almost without a thought she volunteered to have me in her home and to care for me.

I was dumbfounded. There sitting in front of me was a single woman with a demanding job prepared to take on the responsibility of looking after a disabled person who was not related to her. She was a mental health nurse with a position of responsibility within the mental health service. She had an air of authority. I knew it was too much to ask anyone to take up full time care for me. I would not even want to ask that of my own family. However, I found myself accepting her offer. Inwardly I kept saying, 'God there must be a better way.' I was absolutely certain that I did not want to be in a unit for paralysed patients, but how could I burden this young woman.

As a nurse, she was familiar with the procedure of transferring patients internally. Once I accepted her offer she approached the matron. They chatted for a while then they both came over and spoke to me. The offer meant that the hospital plan would be put on hold until the multi agencies for patients' care checked if the proposal made by Dawn was practical. Dawn completed a form of consent and offered dates when the hospital and social service could visit and assess her home as to the suitability of accommodating my disability. In the meantime, I could stay on the ward. Whilst they were checking out Dawn's home, I prayed that it would be difficult to manoeuvre the wheelchair and that something more appropriate would become available. In checking the home, they found that the corridor was too narrow for the smallest wheelchair to pass through so the offer was rejected.

All was not hopeless. Jessica and Eric then offered to have me live with them. It was an attractive proposal. Their home was more accommodating and they had a bookshop where I could help during the day time, and be stimulated by meeting people. Anyway before the multi agencies could arrange the meeting to discuss their offer and carry out the assessment there was an incredible twist, I caught chicken pox. There were spots all over my body, in my ears, face, and every available surface.

It was winter, the weather had suddenly changed and the hospital was bitterly cold. The old and poorly maintained hospital building was not ready for such chronic weather. The elderly patients on the ward were struggling with the extreme cold. At times they were literally blue in their faces. In the evenings during visiting there was uproar as concerned irate family members confronted the hospital staff. They were spitting venom!

I felt sorry for both the families and the staff who were equally victims of the situation. They too had to work in the condition for which they were not in control. But the fact remained that the patients were really suffering. At least the nurses were active and had the opportunity to leave the ward and go home. I was not exempt either. My lower limbs were numb but my arms and chest were sensitive and started to be affected. They were beginning to feel as heavy and numb as the rest of my body, which made managing the wheelchair quite a challenge.

I started to wonder how long it would be before I became unable to wheel myself around. It was a scary thought. At the same time the chickenpox was getting worse. One morning a nurse came to my bed, and said, 'Karlene, your condition is contagious and we have found a room for you. You have to be put in quarantine.'

I was quite indifferent, low in spirit, nothing mattered really. She packed my belongings and I was wheeled along with them into a small side room. Once inside I was really satisfied, it was warm and cosy with a colour television. The warmth and being isolated from the constant disruption and frequent witness of patients dying allowed me to feel safe. It was wonderful, perfect, and peaceful. A sanctuary. There I experienced healing of my mind.

One morning I realised that sensation was returning to my legs. In excitement I called, 'Nurse, Nurse' and as a nurse rushed through the door; 'My legs, my legs, I can feel'. She smiled back as the grin spread across my face.

Then she said, 'I will arrange for you to visit the physiotherapist in the gym tomorrow.' At the crack of dawn I was awake and ready to go to the gym, but I had to work with the programme for the day: firstly to the bathroom followed by breakfast. At last the porter arrived to take me to the gym. He took me along the passages, in and out of lifts, finally into a real gymnasium with lots of equipment. I was supported onto a couch where the physiotherapist thoroughly checked my legs, making notes as he went along. After a full examination, he sat me up with my legs dangling over the side of the couch and explained the regime of exercise he planned for me. During the course of the week I visited the gym a few times.

I was making good progress until the Friday morning. A young nurse took me to the bathroom, hoisted me beyond reach over the bath, and then tried to remove my night clothes. I slid from the security of the seat and was suspended by my fingers on the bar of the chair lift. She managed to lower the chair before I landed from the height into the hard bath. At that stage I was exhausted, frightened and in a total state of shock but I went through the process of being tidied without complaining. However, everything came to a head when I went to the gym. The physiotherapists stood me up, and suddenly I collapsed! I was completely "out". I mean "gone". I guess I was taken back to the ward. Hours later when I woke up I was back in my bed. I was very disappointed. Anyway before the day ended the physiotherapist visited and explained that I had fainted. He thought that perhaps I had worked too hard but at least I had the week-end to recover and could do some gentle exercises in my room until Monday morning.

The rest was good. On Monday I started again. I went from strength to strength, so he introduced me to hydrotherapy. It was incredible. My body felt light and I could do so much more that my confidence grew. Within a few weeks I started to use crutches, standing occasionally and making steps. To me it was a miracle.

The isolation was a tremendous blessing, it allowed me to focus on getting better, undisturbed by the dramas which were a constant feature of the main ward. I don't know how they resolved the dispute over the coldness of the ward, but when I returned it was warmer and calmer. My case was reviewed. The hospital was pleased with the progress I had made and decided that I was well enough to return to the outside world, but needed to be in a ground floor flat. Every effort was made to get a ground floor flat, but they were in short supply. Eventually they decided that my maisonette would suffice if they provided adequate support. I was discharged.

Chapter 7

Transition

Being driven down my street out of the confines of the ward and seeing healthy people moving about and hearing the noise of children playing made me feel at home. The ambulance drew up outside my front door and I was assisted to the sidewalk. No sooner had I got out when neighbours from the house two doors away came to greet me. 'We wondered what became of you,' said one of the ladies.

It was then that I felt embarrassed and thought perhaps I should have sent them a message even though we weren't really close. It was nearly two years since the party of five which included one man and four females had moved into the house. They had excavated their basement and converted it into a church which they called, "Church of God". On several occasions they had invited me, but I really was not interested. I had heard that once you become involved with those church people your life was no longer your own.

Despite my limitations I loved my freedom. I belonged to the United Reformed mainstream church and that was sufficient for me. I must admit I appreciated the warmth which the "Church of God" members exuded and the attention they gave me whenever our paths crossed. We often exchanged greetings across the fence in the back yard and along the street. The children who attended the services on Sundays and during the week were polite and well behaved. Sometimes, seeing the families of African-Caribbean parents and children decked in their Sunday best, walking and talking together, brought back happy memories of my childhood days in Jamaica when I went to church with my grandma and other families. It brought tears to my eyes as I remembered my grandmother. She reared me until the age of twelve, before bringing me to England and returning to Jamaica. Within two years of me living in the UK, she died of cancer. I was not even able to attend her funeral.

The Pastor and two of the ladies who were both sisters and nurses came into the maisonette after the medical staff left me to adjust to my new life. He raised his voice like an angry and concerned father displeased with his wayward daughter, 'Why didn't you get in touch?' I couldn't respond as I hadn't even thought about them. The pained expression on their faces as I explained my experience comforted me. 'Now you are back we give God thanks for your safe return,' he said. The ladies asked me a number of questions pertaining to the care that had been organised by the hospital and social services and told me how they would augment that provision. I was overcome with emotion. I tried desperately not to cry, realising I was now left in the hands of these loving people whom I had rejected in the past. Once the arrangements were made for the next day, they hugged me and streamed through the door with the pastor looking over his shoulder and saying 'Day or night we are at the end of the phone.' I nodded.

From thence the sisters arrived like clock-work every morning, ensuring that I had breakfast, and all my personal needs were met. I had some delicious meals which made me cancel the bland lunches provided by social services.

Living alone was a challenge in itself and having to ascend and descend to the bathroom and kitchen on my bottom like a child made it more painful. Control, control all the way. Balancing against the kitchen counter needed full concentration and reserves of energy, but I was determined. Nevertheless, being at home made my mind less cluttered with thoughts of hopelessness, and the doom and gloom of being institutionalised. Instead I focused on how I would accomplish the next task; coping with my new life! The sisters seemed as if they were never very far away. As well as physically helping me to adjust and manage with the disability, they would spend time talking and listening to me. I felt a part of a family, which motivated me to persevere. Pastor was always entertaining me with jokes and funny expressions as I watched through the upstairs window of the lounge. I had my own street theatre. The ambience, food and care accelerated my progress and each day I got stronger in mind, soul and body.

I missed my son, but I knew it would have been difficult to look after him. At least I was able to phone him often. He was staying in Wolverhampton with my parents. When he came to see me I was really excited, but my spirit was blighted when my mother said, 'Pianki wants to learn so we thought he would be good company and you can teach him.' My heart sank. My thought was, 'How will I manage and what will I do when I have to go for therapy?' I was really quite scared.

Pianki had grown and was even more energetic than before. He pounced about like a young gazelle and was forever asking questions. It was exhausting just watching him racing about the living room. It was difficult dealing with his boundless energy and countless requests at home, but when he went with me to the gym he was like a wild boar who had escaped captivity. It was impossible for me to focus on my activities and the hospital staff were frustrated by his stubbornness. He refused to sit or even just play quietly in the corner. He roved from one end of the gym to the other. I was both angry and embarrassed. Often my muscles got very tense and inhibited my progress.

Each visit was spent trying to get Pianki to calm down. Soon my legs were getting weaker and I found it difficult to stand. I suppressed the urge to bawl for help; after all, Pianki was my only child and he needed me. He could not possibly understand what was happening to his mother. I often grumbled about my predicament to the sisters at the church. One day they said, 'We will arrange for Pianki to stay in our home during your treatment.'

I was overjoyed and extremely grateful. I knew that he would be safe and contented with them as they already spent time reading stories to him. Whenever they stepped into our flat, Pianki would sit them down, switch off the television and sit attentively with a book, eager to receive.

On weekends he attended the Saturday and Sunday schools. He was always keen. The teacher told me that whilst she was teaching, Pianki would sit on the front row mimicking her and making funny faces at her. It frustrated her but she succeeded in maintaining her composure and ensuring that the class was not distracted.

In church he was unable to sit and listen for more than ten minutes. Often Pianki and his friend, Jonathan would position themselves parallel under two rows of chairs, carefully wriggling from the back of the room toward the exit. Then strategically they would manoeuvre themselves from under the chairs and escape through the door. This made me jittery and I wanted to scream out their names. Anyway, the pastor was always ahead and seemed to have had an extra pair of eyes just for them. As they went through the door he would call out, 'Boys are you going somewhere?' Despite his behaviour they were very kind to him. Even the pastor's brother visited regularly in the day to play with him. Eventually Pianki was more settled. I really experienced the love of God, through the pastor and the members of the church, and truly appreciated the love, kindness and support that were given to us.

Chapter 8

Born Again

On Sundays I was collected for church. It was a whole-day affair. After the morning service I was taken to the dining room where I was given a comfortable chair at their dinner table. I felt a little like the Bible character, Mephibosheth, grandson of the first king of Israel, King Saul. As a child he was dropped on his leg causing some deformity. It affected his development and self-confidence. He was not well known but after the death of his father Jonathan, (who was a good friend of King David), he was invited to become a permanent guest at the King's table and inherited all the wealth of his father, and his grandfather, Saul, the previous king.

It was very comforting to be among such loving people and I looked forward to Sundays when I would fellowship with them. When I wasn't focusing on Pianki and all his antics, there was a settled peace inside of me. Mentally I often escaped to somewhere warm, green and calming, usually by the river in Moravia, my district in Jamaica, although I was physically present in the church. The pastor would mention an area and I would have a detailed picture of the event played inside of my mind. The service was lengthy and sometimes I felt a sharp pain in my back and my right leg started to kick forward, spasmodically, but I could not extricate myself from what seemed to me the umbilical cord to real life, direct connection with God.

In September 1987, the year we experienced that violent and destructive hurricane; Pastor Key from Jamaica visited the church. She had a dynamic personality, her voice boomed through the atmosphere commanding the attention of those in the reach of its sound. The first time she visited she was given the opportunity to preach and I found myself trying to catch her every word. She was clear, precise, relevant to our daily lives and quite humorous. I was particularly impressed because for the first time I experienced a confident African-Caribbean woman, who openly and skilfully vacillated between patwa, (the language spoken in Jamaica) and English in a public forum.

I connected with her. To me her delivery was like music to my ears, and it brought back many happy childhood memories of life in Jamaica. Being in her presence gave me a sense of connectedness with my spirituality, racial background and cultural existence. I felt God was now personally interested in me. In fact, Jesus became real, much nearer and tangible. I sat and bathed in the atmosphere, absorbing the teachings. I felt the presence of a force encapsulating me in an energy field. It was protective and comfortable like a body despite being invisible. Suddenly my relationship with God moved from knowing about Him to knowing Him.

Pastor Key was also invited to do some teaching. I was pleased as she brought additional life and vitality to the services. The congregation seemed to have become more vibrant. Two days before the hurricane in October 1987, she instructed the church to fast the following day which would have been a Sunday. During my stay in hospital I was put on a fast before some of the major medical procedures, no food or drink until the tests were completed. 'Why would they want to subject themselves to that?' I wondered.

Anyway no one questioned the instruction and I was curious to know how fasting is done in the church. I decided to participate. Pastor Key told us not to eat or drink any form of beverage from Saturday evening until Sunday evening 6.00 p.m. when the fast would be broken. I arrived at the church early that morning before everyone else and took what had become my regular seat.

The service started on time, as usual. At the end, those who wanted to leave were permitted, and the fasting service began. Scriptures were read with exposition, we sang and were encouraged to pray and worship at intervals. Whilst praying the congregation took up different positions; some sat or laid on the floor, others walked about the room. Due to my limitation I stayed in one position. It became increasingly uncomfortable but I was determined to stay the course.

Pastor Key directed the activities. At times, she called on individuals to pray or read, and songs were started by various members at different intervals. One was never sure what would happen next. The day seemed long and I was beginning to feel both hungry and tired. I could not continue any longer so I decided to go home and rest. I wrestled with the decision before making a move because I felt that it would have been inappropriate for me to stumble out of the service on my crutches in the middle of something so sacred.

I wrote a note for the pastor to explain why I had decided to leave early. I organised myself with my walking aids and respectfully hobbled to the front with the note. As I approached the altar where the pastor stood, the church was singing 'Amazing Grace'; I felt my legs buckling under me and I ended in a neat pile on the floor, still holding the note in my hand. The pastor stood over me. My face was awash with tears, and at the same time I could feel mucus running from my nostrils. I guess I must have looked quite dreadful - good job I am not one for wearing make up.

From that moment I knew (despite my appearance) that I was at peace with God and I felt comfortable with myself. I no longer had that desire to go home. In fact, I felt that the physical hunger pain had faded into insignificance. My life had changed! I would now commit myself to the teaching and life style of the Bible. The detail of the experience on the floor and how I got home remain a mystery.

My next recollection was of myself lying in front of the gas fire as one who was totally in love. It was warm, safe and comfortable. I escaped into a glorious world with bright lights, heavenly music where everything was in harmony and there I spent the night. The following morning, I woke revitalised and rejuvenated with a readiness to face all the challenges life could ever place before me. I almost jumped to my feet from the floor and collided with Pianki who had suddenly come into the room. He seemed extremely calm and self-controlled. We decided to go for an early morning walk.

After having our breakfast and getting dressed we opened the front door. I was aghast. There in front of me were the sturdy London Plane trees which once lined our streets, in disarray. Some were completely uprooted and strewn across the roads, others lent to the right or to the left. There was debris everywhere but no one was in sight; only total devastation. As far as my eyes could see there was damage but I felt at peace. I gently closed the front door and negotiated the steps back to the living room where I sat, trying to figure out what had happened.

The mystery was soon to be unravelled when the news came on the radio. A hurricane had swept through the country destroying buildings and uprooting trees. Even Kew Gardens that was once the heart of Britain's botanical attraction had been completely blown to the ground. As I listened to what happened during the night reality struck home, my mouth dropped open and I mentally escaped from the room. When I re-entered I lifted my hands and praised God because I was convinced that He had shielded me during the storm. I felt assured that He will always protect me. That caused me to smile.

Chapter 9

An unexpected relationship

Whilst Pastor Key was still in England she continued to frequent our church. She had made an appeal for support of the families who became homeless from the 1986 flood that had occurred in Jamaica. She also requested financial donations to build their church. Her mission was based on supporting the underprivileged community in St. Catherine, Jamaica. She had a heart for young men, taking them out of the ghetto and providing the opportunity for a better life. The young men were achieving in school and the seniors were developing new skills including building their church in St. Catherine, Jamaica. Her effort engaged my interest and I felt eager to become involved. I knew that physically and financially I was limited, but I wanted to do whatever was possible, so I went home and sorted out some of Pianki's clothes for the children and a small financial gift for the building funds.

During the week, I asked Cynthia (one of the sisters from the church) who was now like family, if she would accompany me to Pastor Key. She welcomed the idea, and thought it would be therapeutic. We set out on the journey. Needless to say Pianki was excited, and he needed a rein to stop him from disappearing. I was very slow, but Cynthia was patient. Snail-paced I inched my way, whilst Cynthia managed to keep track of Pianki. At last we reached the block of flats. We had to climb two flights of steps to get to Pastor Key's maisonette. It was no easy feat getting up those steps, but I made it, breathless, exhausted with two tired legs. I could have sat at the top of the steps, but was encouraged to do the length of the corridor when Cynthia gently placed her left hand under my right arm.

On the first knock Pastor Key opened the door having seen us passing her kitchen window. She greeted us with warm embraces. Pianki jumped into her arms; she held him tightly and told him how much she loved him. The room was full of her laughter and jokes. I felt a genuine attraction towards her.

There was another lady standing just behind Pastor Key. She had visited the church but I never had the opportunity to greet her. As I stood next to her I felt uncomfortable. She stared intensely into my face. To ease the tension, I spoke, extending my hand, 'Hello, I am Karlene.'

She stared even more and it felt like a laser beam cutting through my flesh. Then she spoke. I was jolted by the sudden sound, 'Whey yu name again?'

I repeated, 'Karlene'.

'Nooah, nooah whey dey used to call you?'

Without hesitation 'Mackie', I said.

Almost moved to tears, she blurted out

'A wha mek yu so ugly'.

I froze, feeling frightened and ashamed. The lady turned to Pastor Key saying,

'Mom, Mom she used to be such a pretty little girl with hair down in her back.' Turning her gaze to me again she said, 'A wey dey do to yu.'

The look on the pastor's face showed that she was just as puzzled as I was. I wanted to crawl under a chair. 'Mish' said Pastor but before she could finish the lady continued,

'Mom, mom wi from de same district. Mom, she is Miss Grace grand daughta. Mi used to plait her hair and sometimes she stay a mi house.' My heart started to race. I looked at the lady hoping to remember her face but my mind was blank. I could not recall her, yet everything that she spoke about me was true - my name, my grandparents and having my hair plaited at the home she described.

The whole situation was remarkable, too remarkable for me to accept that it was an accident or a coincidence. I was convinced that God had brought Pastor Key in my life for a purpose and this lady, (her missionary) was the link. It had to be a divine plan. The rest of the visit was full of stories of my childhood and the powerful influence of my grandma in the community. I wanted to cry but forced back the tears. Instead I just listened and laughed. My grandma had died in Jamaica whilst I was studying in Yorkshire. I was unable to attend the funeral so there was a lot of spiritual growth and arranged the trip for Pianki and me. I looked forward to the event. Something new, something different in my life! I was curious and welcomed the break after being stuck at home. Since my discharge from hospital my time was spent between the church, the gym and home. I often reminisced of the times when I used to play squash, go out with friends and sometimes dance. I mourned the loss of the ability to be very active.

The opportunity to be in Wales, a particular beauty spot for me where I had studied marine biology, was exciting. I loved the open space, gentle hills covered with shrubs, grass and other vegetation, the valleys and the sea which embroidered the mainland. Furthermore, I would be doing different things and meeting new people. I counted each day until it was time to go. The thought of a whole week away with Pianki would be good, especially the fresh air and open space for him to run about freely.

At last it was time to depart. Our party consisting of a family with grandma, mother, two boys and a girl nearing Pianki's age, a single young lady, Pianki and I, boarded the coach. We sat close to each other. The drive was long but the time passed quite quickly. When we arrived at the camp site it was very bright and hot. Although it was getting late the sun shone brightly. When I alighted from the coach I was taken aback with the vast Butlins holiday camp site that I could see stretching for miles. The whole site was dedicated to Christian meetings for the week. I had given no thought as to who would be in attendance, but I must admit I was surprised and shocked when a sea of white faces interspersed with specks of colour here and there.

Everything was extremely orderly, no unruly children, neat lines of people, some in clusters making their way to their allocated chalets. A steward led us to our chalet. It was basic self catering accommodation, humble but clean. Once we unpacked we set off to the first meeting which I was eager to attend, especially since the needs of the children had been adequately catered for. The children were guided to their sessions. I entered the large auditorium, it was almost full, hundreds of people were already seated whilst the rest of us were being directed to our seats. As I Looked around, everyone within my vision seemed to have had a look of serenity while basking in the music that filled the atmosphere.

Everyday there were three sessions starting with early morning prayer meeting, followed by a midday session and the evening service. At the spiritual growth and arranged the trip for Pianki and me. I looked forward to the event. Something new, something different in my life! I was curious and welcomed the break after being stuck at home. Since my discharge from hospital my time was spent between the church, the gym and home. I often reminisced of the times when I used to play squash, go out with friends and sometimes dance. I mourned the loss of the ability to be very active.

The opportunity to be in Wales, a particular beauty spot for me where I had studied marine biology, was exciting. I loved the open space, gentle hills covered with shrubs, grass and other vegetation, the valleys and the sea which embroidered the mainland. Furthermore, I would be doing different things and meeting new people. I counted each day until it was time to go. The thought of a whole week away with Pianki would be good, especially the fresh air and open space for him to run about freely.

At last it was time to depart. Our party consisting of a family with grandma, mother, two boys and a girl nearing Pianki's age, a single young lady, Pianki and I, boarded the coach. We sat close to each other. The drive was long but the time passed quite quickly. When we arrived at the camp site it was very bright and hot. Although it was getting late the sun shone brightly. When I alighted from the coach I was taken aback with the vast Butlins holiday camp site that I could see stretching for miles. The whole site was dedicated to Christian meetings for the week. I had given no thought as to who would be in attendance, but I must admit I was surprised and shocked when a sea of white faces interspersed with specks of colour here and there.

Everything was extremely orderly, no unruly children, neat lines of people, some in clusters making their way to their allocated chalets. A steward led us to our chalet. It was basic self catering accommodation, humble but clean. Once we unpacked we set off to the first meeting which I was eager to attend, especially since the needs of the children had been adequately catered for. The children were guided to their sessions. I entered the large auditorium, it was almost full, hundreds of people were already seated whilst the rest of us were being directed to our seats. As I Looked around, everyone within my vision seemed to have had a look of serenity while basking in the music that filled the atmosphere.

Everyday there were three sessions starting with early morning prayer meeting, followed by a midday session and the evening service. At the crack of dawn we were up, ready and eager to go. Mother Cave, the grandmother of the family was the first. We were woken by her joyous, melodious singing. It was a joy to be in her presence as she was a great encourager for all of us.

There was a wonderful spirit in our chalet. The children were cooperative and obedient. Everyone took on a role of responsibility to ensure that the chalet was kept tidy and we ate healthily. Pianki fitted in and behaved in a responsible way.

Each day was fresh and exciting, I almost ran to the sessions, not wanting to miss anything. Children were well cared for. I cannot remember them being rude and unruly, or parents shouting or any litter strewn about. Wherever you looked there were clusters of people praying, or walking and talking about spiritual things. Some greeted each other with hugs and kisses. Everyone emanated radiance. It was a beautiful sight.

In our Bible study I had learned that the true witness of having a relationship with God was the manifestation of love, peace, joy, meekness, gentleness, goodness, self-control, longsuffering and faithfulness which were collectively know as fruits of the Holy Spirit of God. As I Walked around the camp I felt that the people displayed the fruit of the Holy Spirit. I also felt that it was being manifested in my life as there was much peace inside of me and I had become much more patient, gentle and kind.

At one particular evening meeting the guest speaker was Nicky Cruz, the writer and international speaker, known for the book the "Cross and the Switch Blade" which depicted his life. Nicky was accompanied by his co-writer, David Wilkinson. As usual the auditorium was absolutely packed with thousands of people. There was a slight hum intermingled with the music, in preparation for Nicky. When he stood to speak, there was uproar followed by total hush as we listened and every fibre of my being held on to the words as they exited his mouth.

Nicky had been a member of a violent street gang. One day whilst creating havoc he was captivated by the singing coming from a nearby church in the community. He was drawn into the building by an overwhelming force. When Nicky approached the door a well dressed woman adorned with a broad hat which obscured the inside of the building tried to stop him from entering, but he was insistent and pushing her to one side, he entered the church. He went to the altar where he confessed his sin, asked

God for forgiveness and accepted that God was his Lord and Saviour. At that point Nicky became a "Born Again" Christian. That was the beginning of a life changing journey, a journey he was still on.

After Nicky Cruse shared his testimony, a pastor preached and then requested that all those who believed that God had called them to become missionaries to travel the world to help others, should come forward to the altar. Without thinking, I got up from my seat and like a mannequin moved to the rostrum propelled forward quite swiftly by the mass of people who responded. I stood directly under the platform which stood higher than most people. I felt I was covered by a big rock and within moments a strange babbling flowed from my mouth. It went on and on and on. I seemed not to be in control. Then it stopped. I wasn't sure what was said by the pastor during the time I stood at the platform, but I was convinced in my heart and mind that I would spend the rest of my life going around the world helping others. When the babbling stopped I went back to my seat knowing that I had made a commitment to give my life over to such work.

The following day I went to a workshop in the afternoon where people were being invited to wait for the gift of "speaking in tongues". I wanted to speak in tongues even though I wasn't sure what it meant. I took a seat with the rest of the people and the leader prayed, thanking God for what He was about to do in the meeting. Immediately I started to babble in the strange language that took control of me the previous night at the altar. The leader came by my side and started to thank God for blessing me with tongues. It was then I understood what had happened to me at the rostrum.

After the session I went to the bookshop where I bought a book on the baptism of the Holy Spirit to have a better understanding of what was happening to me. It was clear from my experience that I was truly "Born Again" and the Spirit of God was within me.

I felt different and I wanted to spend the rest of my life in the camp. When the adults in my party suggested that we should take the children for a walk into the town, I was horrified; I abhorred the thought, but managed to disguise my feeling. 'I murmured to myself, 'How can we pollute ourselves with ungodly things?' Inwardly I had become very sanctimonious.

That afternoon we went for a walk. The children were excited. They played along the side walk as the adults strolled at a steady pace, stopping at intervals to window-shop and to take in the natural beauty of the little village. To be perfectly honest, I was distracted, my body was there, but everything else was in the camp. At last they decided to turn back, as the little ones were getting tired and hungry. My heart leapt with joy.

The rest of the week was full of activities. I hardly had time to check out the range of resources at the bookstalls. I attended all the evening meetings and some of the workshops throughout the days. The time went quickly and soon we were on our way home. I was bubbling with excitement, eager to share my new life with everyone. The time spent in Minehead marked the beginning of a new chapter in my life.

Chapter 10

He speaks, why not sensitise your ears?

GOD had spoken to me on several occasions. At first I thought that I was suffering from an over-active imagination. My first vivid recollection was in early June of 1987. It was a Sunday morning and I was sitting in the church next door. It was really the basement of the house which had been converted into a small church to accommodate about sixty people. The pastor was in a rather jovial mood. He started the service by asking how many of the members were only present in body, but their minds were in the Caribbean. I smiled to myself because just before his interruption my mind and spirit were not in that room. There was a voice saying to me 'On the 24th of June go to Jamaica for a while. There your mind will be restored.' Immediately I felt the warmth of the Caribbean breeze on my face, heard the richness of the language and smelled the aromas of the island of Jamaica. I looked around to see if anyone else was privy to the same experience, but they were standing with their hands raised to the sky, some with their eyes closed. Everyone was praising and worshipping God as they always did in this first part of the service.

Relieved that no one had noticed that I had escaped from the room, I smiled to myself. Then the thought came that God might have revealed what I was doing to the pastor, and at that moment I felt foolish, perhaps a little embarrassed. Suddenly I felt a surge of heat in my body which made me restless, I looked sheepishly to the flooring avoiding eye contact with the pastor or other members. I wanted to disappear from the room, to be alone. Tears started to well up in my eyes. I was feeling depressed and alone. The day passed and I settled back into my routine.

I had put that experience to the back of my mind until the most incredible thing happened. After the 24th of June which was my sister's birthday, my mum phoned and after chatting for a while she said, Karlene, 'Why didn't you go to Jamaica for a break, I would have paid for you. I am sure the change would have done you good.' Then she laughed. I guess she would not even recall saying that, but I noted it into a journal. For some reason once I started to develop my finer movements I kept a journal. I felt it was something I had to do. It was not regular, but was a prompt to record certain experiences, emotions, thoughts, feelings and events.

This was followed by another unusual incident, two days later I had a letter from my grand aunt who lived in Kingston, Jamaica. I had not heard from her for many years and had not seen her since leaving Jamaica in 1967. In the letter she implied that I could have visited and stayed with her. Everything seemed so bizarre. Both my mother and my grand aunt wrote and spoke about what I could have done without giving me the option to do it. I kept it all to myself only sharing with my faithful journal which had become a silent friend. It would not laugh at me or make me feel ashamed.

The following year, around June or July, I am not sure of the exact date this time as it was not recorded; I was in the same spot in the church when I heard the same voice again. The message remained the same. This time I took note of the instructions. I determined to book the flight, believing that my mother would pay for it and my grand aunt would provide the accommodation. The following day I reserved two tickets to Jamaica. I did not think it was necessary to discuss it with my mother being convinced that God had already prepared both my mom and grand aunt to play their part in Pianki and me travelling to Jamaica that summer. I was excited about the trip. There was a warm comforting feeling inside.

By now my physical health had improved and I could get around without crutches, albeit slowly. My thinking and reasoning capacity were widening and my self confidence had grown. I started to do sessional adult literacy classes for the local Further Education College. The pay was just adequate to cover all my expenses; entertainment and travel abroad was a luxury that I could not afford. Anyway, by faith I booked the tickets. The agency gave me a deadline by which to pay the money. Shortly after I had reserved the tickets, I was asked by the college to teach adult literacy using the computer. At the time I had just started to use computers. I explained to my employer that I was inexperienced and my knowledge was limited. But it didn't seem to matter. They insisted, so I took on the challenge. I one of the older sisters, visited unexpectedly. She came with a purpose, wanting to know all about what was being arranged by the hospital. This was unusual because she was neither family nor a close friend. Anyway I shared what the hospital had decided to do. Almost without a thought she volunteered to have me in her home and to care for me.

I was dumbfounded. There sitting in front of me was a single woman with a demanding job prepared to take on the responsibility of looking after a disabled person who was not related to her. She was a mental health nurse with a position of responsibility within the mental health service. She had an air of authority. I knew it was too much to ask anyone to take up full time care for me. I would not even want to ask that of my own family. However, I found myself accepting her offer. Inwardly I kept saying, 'God there must be a better way.' I was absolutely certain that I did not want to be in a unit for paralysed patients, but how could I burden this young woman.

As a nurse, she was familiar with the procedure of transferring patients internally. Once I accepted her offer she approached the matron. They chatted for a while then they both came over and spoke to me. The offer meant that the hospital plan would be put on hold until the multi agencies for patients' care checked if the proposal made by Dawn was practical. Dawn completed a form of consent and offered dates when the hospital and social service could visit and assess her home as to the suitability of accommodating my disability. In the meantime, I could stay on the ward. Whilst they were checking out Dawn's home, I prayed that it would be difficult to manoeuvre the wheelchair and that something more appropriate would become available. In checking the home, they found that the corridor was too narrow for the smallest wheelchair to pass through so the offer was rejected.

All was not hopeless. Jessica and Eric then offered to have me live with them. It was an attractive proposal. Their home was more accommodating and they had a bookshop where I could help during the day time, and be stimulated by meeting people. Anyway before the multi agencies could arrange the meeting to discuss their offer and carry out the assessment there was an incredible twist, I caught chicken pox. There were spots all over my body, in my ears, face, and every available surface.

It was winter, the weather had suddenly changed and the hospital was bitterly cold. The old and poorly maintained hospital building was not ready for such chronic weather. The elderly patients on the ward were

Chapter 11

The journey began

The flight was via Miami Florida. We had to wait in the departure lounge for the connecting flight, it was lengthy, and seemed unending. Pianki amused himself by playing in and out of the seats. I stood next to an expansive sheet of glass which extended from one side of the waiting lounge separating the passengers inside from the planes on the runway. I tried to distract myself from Pianki's activities by looking at the shapes, colours and markings on the planes; nevertheless, there was a watchful eye to make sure he did not wander off.

For a split second I took my eyes off him and focused on a plane that had just landed. It seemed that from nowhere a woman came and sat on one of the seats. As Pianki played she spoke to him, and soon he slowed his pace and became absorbed in the conversation. I cocked my ear to funnel in every word. I heard when she said 'I am going to the rain forest, where are you going?' Pianki said Jamaica. Then she asked, 'What is your name?' He looked directly at her. To my amazement he said 'Mark Rickard.' My mouth gaped and I looked toward them. He took his gaze from the woman and looked at me intensely as if to say mom don't you dare say otherwise. With embarrassment I looked away. His response troubled me, why has he changed his name and why Mark? As I looked through the glass I could see their reflection because the plane had now been positioned so that a section of the glass appeared like a mirror. I used my camera that I had draped around my neck and took a photograph of the reflection of myself on the side of one of the planes.

At last it was time to board the plane for Jamaica. When everyone was comfortably seated the plane taxied along the runway and we were airborne. It had barely levelled off in the sky before we descended and landed. The journey was short, in fact shorter than the wait had been.

I was glad to be home it had been a long day. I was eager to be met and taken home. It had been about twenty years since I had seen my grand aunt so I wasn't sure I would be able to recognise her, but at least I had sent her a picture of us. I had not thought that the picture may have gone astray and she would not be there to meet us. But I was getting concerned. The plane had landed and having cleared customs very quickly we were now in the arrival lounge where the atmosphere was lively and exciting. Many people were bustling about, relatives and friends greeting each other. In the background there was a melody of sweet music from the night creatures. The heat was intense and natural light had faded leaving pitch blackness with patches of illuminated areas where the street lamps stood tall. I was dazed by all the activities and felt overwhelmed and nervous. I looked in every direction hoping that my grand aunt would see us and come to take us home.

We stood just outside the ice-cream parlour but that was a bad idea. Pianki wanted an ice-cream, but I had no Jamaican currency. He started to whine. I understood his craving. It had been a long time since we had eaten and the ice-cream was really tempting. His behaviour made me feel even more desperate for my grand aunt to arrive. He was hyperactive at the best of times but was much worse in the present situation.

Visitors, friends and relatives were being collected, the crowd got less dense, the vehicles were fewer and the heat seemed more direct.

'Oh God' I muttered to myself as my stomach started to churn. Fear gripped me. Where was my grand aunt? I thought.

It was getting darker and darker. I was really confused, what could I do? Then I thought of Professor Golding, who was a bone specialist at the university hospital. We had become acquainted in 1979 when I visited the island. He and his wife, also a doctor, were very hospitable and had given an open invitation to visit. This was far from being an appropriate time, but I was desperate. I reached for my address book and walked into the telephone kiosk which was next to us. 'Oh no,' I said when I remembered I had no Jamaican currency. The man standing nearby must have heard my cry and seen the despair on my face.

'Can I help?' he asked. I explained. He listened, then took a telephone card from his pocket and handed it to me. I took it and went back into the call box. He watched as I tried to make the call.

After several unsuccessful attempts, I was startled as he came behind me. 'Let me help.' I stepped aside making room for him. He took the address book and dialled the number. It seemed so simple yet I had struggled. He stepped out handing me the receiver whilst the phone was ringing. It rang for a while then a local voice, said, 'Goodnight'.

'Goodnight, can I speak to Professor Golding, please' I said.

The voice came back, 'He has left for Scotland with his family on vacation'.

My heart sank. 'Thank you.'

I replaced the receiver and came out of the call box being careful not to show that I was petrified. We were all alone. I looked to the man, trying to be brave, 'Thank you very much sir.' I said. He smiled and walked off.

I could hear my heart beating faster and felt my legs getting quite heavy and my brain was on fire. I desperately needed a solution. I looked at the bags against the wall and Pianki sitting on one of the cases, by now he was looking tired. I felt discouraged and searched for an answer. The only safe option was to report to the police station which was a short distance away. It was about nine o'clock, some two hours since we came out of the airport. It felt like eternity. I was about to gather the bags when I remembered that Pianki wanted an ice cream. The least I could do was buy one for him. He must have been very hungry. I hoped they would accept the British currency. I was about to go into the ice-cream kiosk when I looked into the distance. Now that it was no longer thronged with people and vehicles moving in and out, I could see quite far into the distance. To my amazement I saw what I thought was the figure of Pastor Key with a man. I peered intensely hoping to see more clearly. They were walking toward us. As the figures got closer, I saw that familiar grin of Pastor Key. I knew who it was but I had to wonder was this reality or just a dream.

Within minutes she was embracing me, Pianki regained his energy and she moved quickly to pick him up. I looked as she held my child. I was so grateful, I wanted to swing from her neck and plaster her face with kisses, but somehow I didn't think that would be appropriate so I restrained myself. Instead I kept smiling as I looked at them. The gentleman who accompanied her was one of her deacons. They had come directly from the church in Spanish Town, to collect me. I don't know if we talked about my grand aunt at that point but I was very happy and relieved to get into that motor car. Once the cases were loaded Pianki and I sat comfortably on the back seat and we set off for her home some sixty odd miles away in Clarendon. On the way we stopped at the deacon's home which was near the church; about twenty miles from the airport. Although it was quite late his home was a hive of activities, his wife sewing, children playing and adults talking. We were introduced to everyone. One of the ladies gave me a mango. I held the large kidney shaped fruit in my left hand and ran my right hand over the smooth skin; I could smell the sweet fragrance. The atmosphere, and warm welcome gave me a real sense of belonging. It took me back to my early childhood in Moravia.

After a brief stop we drove for about an hour and a half to Pastor Key's home. The journey was surrounded by pitch darkness interspersed with streaks of white lines from the electric bulbs of the few houses we passed and stars in the distant night sky. The atmosphere was pregnant with sounds of crickets, owls and a variety of singing animals. As the car turned into the gateway, the gates were opened by an elderly man who I learned was Pastor Key's uncle. The car cruised into the drive way by the side of the house. It stopped close to the doorway to the side entrance of the house so that I would not have to walk far.

I opened the car door and pulled my tired pained body to an upright position by holding on to the opened door. I stretched and breathed deeply. The warm fresh air bathed my face and filled my lungs. Pianki followed me. We climbed into the passage. Pastor Key showed us into a room almost immediately from the entrance. It was a spacious room tastefully furnished with a fragrance of lemon polish. The bed was well made in matching pastel shades and the well polished dresser reflected the light from the bulb. I flopped on the bed, so did Pianki. It was comfortable. We had a good night's rest.

Chapter 12

Who can understand?

After resting at Pastor Key's home for a day the deacon's son took Pianki and me into Kingston to look for my grand aunt's home. It took us a while to find the house which was tucked away behind another house. There was more than one house sharing the same plot of land. It was an area of high deprivation and crime. What a shock it was! I suddenly realised how much at risk Pianki and I would have been that night had I decided to take a taxi to search for my grand aunt's home when she was not at the airport to meet us. I breathed a sigh of relief and whispered words of gratitude to God.

After that initial shock I accepted the situation and was prepared to stay with my grand aunt but somehow it did not happen. Instead Pastor Key's home in May Pen became our home for the next eight years. However, Pianki and I visited my grand aunt regularly. We got to know the people in the neighbourhood and they got to know us. Despite the violence we felt safe. At least I did. On one occasion my cousin and I were going to a gospel service which was held in a tent in the neighbouring district. We took a short cut. As we went along the winding foot path, there lying in the grass was a figure. It was a dead man. I panicked, but my cousin just took it in his stride. That was a common occurrence in the area. When I slept their over-night, the atmosphere was often pierced with sounds of gun shots. Many years later my grand aunt lost her eldest son who was shot when he went to purchase something from the shop, never returning home alive to his wife and newly born twins.

During the daytime the children played along the streets and in the yard while adults talked about the killings and robberies as they went about their daily routines. The small dwelling places were almost on top of each other so there was no privacy. I strolled around with ease, trusting God to look after us. I made sure I dressed modestly without jewellery, not even my watch. Despite the level of poverty, the people were warm, friendly and kind. Pianki had a great time playing with the children. There was a real sense of community. With their limited resources they shared what they had with each other.

Chapter 13

Restoration

The stay in Jamaica helped me to get my life into perspective physically, spiritually and emotionally. Going back to my roots I felt a oneness with the environment. The language, food and people were familiar. I was able to speak freely using my first language Patwa which gave me a sense of identity and positive regard. I could express myself easily without feeling embarrassed and misunderstood. The people understood me and I them. To see Pianki in the open space playing and interacting with other children made me less tense and stressed. I shared his care with members in the church. They were very supportive. The food, sunshine and regular walks on the uneven pavement and rough paths made me stronger and healthier. At last I started to think positively about having a future.

The first Sunday at Pastor Key's newly-built wooden church I was invited to address the people in the church. I walked confidently to the front, turned, looked and scanned all the beautiful faces that had greeted us earlier. I took a deep breath and the words flowed from my mouth. With each delivery I felt as if shackles were being released from my mind. 'Free at last, Free at last.' I uttered within.

With those words I wanted to jump, skip and dance. I felt I had found myself - my identity. The Karlene that had got lost in the sea of cultural diversity in England, without a voice or a song to sing, had been restored. I felt ready to return to my native land. It was where I wanted to live. I could see no reason to return to England. No regular employment and poor health were hardly any credentials to keep me there. Moreover, Pianki had taken well to the island; he adjusted to the people and climate and loved the food. I made up my mind to look for a job.

Carefully pursuing the job section of the national Sunday paper, The Gleaner, I saw the advert for the Head of Biological Science for Mico Teachers' Training College, a prestigious college. I read the specification through and through. I was convinced that it was tailor-made for me. I had the required qualifications and skills and I felt ready to take on the demands and responsibilities of the post. I was eager. In my mind I was actually enjoying the prestige and the perks of the post and the thought of never being cold again. I said to myself in a proud and arrogant way, 'Me, Karlene, Head of Biological Science at Mico Teacher's Training College.'

The following day I made contact with the office and requested an application form. Having completed and submitted the form I shared my success with God and went to the church for prayer. Certainly not the right order. I really should have asked God for direction. Later in that week I visited with my grand aunt. I could not wait to tell her what I had decided to do, pointing out my new position at Mico with all the benefits for Pianki and me.

Chapter 14

The vision

The heat coupled with the excitement exhausted me so I went and curled up on her bed, looking up at the ceiling. As I lay there, as though watching a cinema screen, I could see a series of animated scenes of which I was a part. Firstly, I was in the Principal's office sitting before him and another gentleman. They were asking me a number of questions about my experience, qualifications and reason for being in Jamaica. It was more like a friendly exchange than an interview. They kept smiling and nodding as I spoke freely. After the chat I was shown around the main building, the library and then the laboratories. In the main lab there was a young man of light complexion with hair shortly cropped, possibly in his thirties, leaning against one of the benches. He was a technician. He looked at me and nodded. It felt as if he had welcomed me into the post.

We returned to the office where I was asked a couple more questions and then given the opportunity to ask questions. There and then the job was offered. Before I could say anything there was an overriding voice which said 'Don't take it.' Immediately the ceiling came back into focus. The experience unnerved me and I rose from the bed and went to sit in the doorway next to my grand aunt.
'Yu com back already' she said continuing to look outside at Pianki running about in front of the house. I must have delayed in responding as she repeated herself. Then I told her what I saw.
'Wonda what da mean' she said.
I guess we were both wondering. Two days later I received a letter from the college inviting me for an interview.

At the interview the vision replayed. I almost had a heart attack when I went into the laboratory. It was too real. There was that familiar scene with the familiar face and position of the technician leaning against the bench! My heart raced and I perspired profusely. My temperature must have exceeded the limits of the thermometer. I wanted to run out of the lab. During the rest of the tour I felt numb. It was a relief to return to the office, hopefully to sit and relax but there was no time for that because the questions started immediately. In spite of everything I was confident that I had done enough to get the job.

The Principal thanked me for coming and said that if they should offer me the post I would need my certificates from England. However, there were other candidates to be interviewed before a decision could be made. He advised me to telephone the following Tuesday, as there was no telephone at my residence and they could not contact me by phone. I rose from the chair, shook their hands and left the room. I knew the church was praying and everyone wanted me to stay, especially the deacon who collected us from the airport. They had remarked how well I looked since being on the island. Pastor Key had strong faith. She was sure that the job was mine and had made arrangements for me to stay with a member of the church who lived quite near the college.

The following Tuesday I rang. The principal answered, 'Miss Rickard we would like to offer you the post. If you decide to accept you need to send us your certificates.' By now I was confident about getting the job, but hearing the offer still came as a surprise. I remained silent for a while. I felt tears welling up in my eyes. I wanted to shout and tell the whole world about my success. I felt six feet tall. My thought was, 'Imagine little insignificant me as The Head of Biological Science in the most prestigious teachers' college in Jamaica'. I was excited. Finally, I was jolted back to reality when the principal said, 'Miss Rickard, what is your decision?'

I stuttered. I was close to saying yes, the offer was too good to refuse. The status, financial help to secure a mortgage, purchase a car and support Pianki in an excellent prep school, what more could I have wanted? Then the vision knocked on the door of my memory and my thoughts were thrown into turmoil. I was tormented. I heard myself saying, 'I will phone you with my decision tomorrow, sir.'

The passage of time did not make it any easier especially as Pastor Key and those with whom I shared couldn't understand my indecision. It caused me to question the vision, 'How could the Lord not want me to have this job?' I became quite angry with Him.

The following day I could not find the strength to make that telephone call so I decided to wait a little longer before making up my mind. Whilst deciding I reflected on my life's journey remembering how God had taken me out of very difficult situations and provided for me when no one was available. He had been the best friend I ever had and had been responsible for bringing different people into my life. I came to the conclusion that I had to be obedient. In the Bible it is stated that obedience is better than sacrifice. I felt God was calling me to be obedient and have total faith in Him. Immediately, I decided to refuse the position. I told Pastor Key. She was disappointed, but accepted my decision. Friday morning, I phoned the principal and declined the position. From his tone he sounded angry. I assumed that other favoured candidates may have moved on which made me feel guilty, but as I replaced the receiver there was a settled peace within me.

Chapter 15

Hurricane Gilbert

The Sunday when Pianki and I should have left Jamaica after a life changing holiday, Gilbert came. We attended the morning service. I cannot be sure of the time but as I stood in the churchyard the atmosphere seemed eerie and sinister. I looked up into the sky. I noticed that it started to change. The beautiful bright blue sky gradually changed to a fiery burning red. My eyes were transfixed; I reached for my camera, and zoomed in on the sky. Around me it was so still; not a voice or even natural sounds. Suddenly the lens was covered by a dense blackness. I zoomed out to give a wider view. It was dark around and visibility was poor.

Suddenly the atmosphere changed, there was a rushing wind. The breeze was fierce, but cool; sinister and eerie. Minute by minute it gathered speed like a convoy of vehicles tumbling from a precipice. It was brisk. The air felt sharp to my face. I can't remember how we got to the senior missionary's house which was about ten minutes walk from the church. But there we were our pastor, her husband (the deacon), a couple of brethren and the missionary's family. We were imprisoned in the house by the howling wind. Everyone stood on the grilled veranda and stared into the openness daring not to venture outside. The children were excited, jumping up and down and shouting. The missionary's only daughter, out of five children, was ecstatic. 'Oh, she said, I have never experienced a hurricane before and I always wanted to.' She was in her late teens. She stood, held on to the grill and positioned her head through a gap and watched intently with anticipation.

From our sanctuary we all watched Hurricane Gilbert, the dreaded one, rampage the street, tossing trees from side to side. A tall coconut tree was literally flattened on the ground away from the house, but as the wind changed direction the tree was lifted high, it stood tall and straight like a giant surveying the land; then it lay down again on the opposite side, an animated tree behaving like an animal. The sheets of zinc from the house and surrounding houses flew through the air like tissue paper.

Despite all the violent activity outside, there seemed to be a sort of stillness - isolation. We were cut off from the rest of Jamaica except for the voice which filled my ear from my bright yellow walkman radio and tape. Everyone waited on me for the next news report. It made me feel important. I listened with a sense of pride. I used my hand to secure the ear piece, to make sure I did not miss any of the news. After all I was the only contact between the household and the outside world. I listened closely and excitedly. I shared the news, albeit about devastations and the hopelessness of the situation. Jamaica was out of control. I guess like the missionary's daughter who desperately wanted the experience I was full of the moment being purposeful; being functional, a point of respect.

There was devastation everywhere over the island. We could no longer see anything on the outside; the day had merged into the night. As the darkness intensified every minute seemed like a hundred days. During the night the beating of the rain on the roof was like a stampede of wild bulls. The breeze sounded fiercer, demolishing the surrounding areas. There was that informative voice at my ear asking us to remain calm and not to go outside. She detailed all that was happening across the island. I shared the news, being careful not to omit anything.

After a long night we woke to a calmer day. There were spells of lull between the breezes, noticeable by the movement of the trees. It was drizzling. During the breaks, the strong, brave young men in the house, along with two more from the house next door mounted the roofs of their houses and the neighbouring houses, in order to secure the zinc with some building blocks that were around. They were quick, skilful and alert. Soon they decked the roofs with blocks and were back into the sanctuary of the house. With time the wind subsided. The most incredible thing happened. There was a sudden full stop, no rain, no breeze. One would never believe that there had been such a terrible storm but for the experience and the evidence both outside and inside of the house. However, I kept tuned into the radio. The reporter emphasized, 'Please do not leave your homes. The storm has not finished. It is not safe outside; storm is still in the air. We will keep you informed of further developments.' I was careful to tell the household.

Before the last word had left my mouth my pastor was almost through the gates, followed by the deacon and his son. He was one of the young men that had been helping to repair the roofs in the neighbourhood. I quickly rushed after them with my camera around my neck and the radio attached to my ear. We all piled into the deacon's car. I kept in tune with the outside world and reported everything to my now intimate group. We really should not have been outside. But we were. When the road became impassable, we got out of the car. As we wandered from place to place there was total devastation. Houses were collapsed! Trees and pavement were uprooted and there was flooding. The contents of houses and shops were strewn everywhere. There were men pushing hand carts with furniture they never owned before - beds and dressers and even sheets of zinc. The reporter was painting the same picture across the island.

My pastor visited the brethren in different areas just to check that they were okay. People approached us, mostly looking at me. They loudly poured out their woes, competing with each other. I guess they thought I was a reporter or someone from the government who would be able to alleviate their situation. Some wanted me to photograph their plight - the contents of their houses outside. We were paralysed with hopelessness. All we could do was to encourage them to stay inside but for some there really was not much of an inside. When we passed the church it was split in two, all that hard work that the brethren had put into erecting such a beautiful building over the last few weeks seemed wasted. But at that point I was busy thanking God, because we could have been in the church.

I was jolted to reality when the reporter gave a warning that the second phase of the storm was on its way. I relayed it to the party. We made our way back to the house. We had just got inside when the rage started again. It sounded worse than the first phase. First the wind, then the rain, it poured like the Niagara Falls, filling the space in front of the house. I felt like we were in a giant pool. The water started to rise around the house. Even the deacon's once-excited daughter got frightened and cried for it to stop. It was a frightening sight. The house was like a sinking ship, as the water got higher and higher. I looked through the bars of the grill until everything faded into oblivion. By now everything in the house had stopped working. The stench of the bathroom was unbearable. There was plenty of water outside but none inside to flush the toilet. Even drinking water was reduced.

Later that day the hand of God stilled the rain, but for a light drizzle, and slight breeze. The water level on the outside of the house started to drop. Thanks be to God we were still there. The hurricane went on for days. On the Wednesday when things were much calmer we visited the house of the pastor, some twenty miles away in May Pen, to check on other members of her family and her friends. At that point people were breathing a sigh of relief and gathering what they could. It was distressing for everyone. It was a miracle that Pastor Key's house was virtually untouched. Although There was an enormous breadfruit tree at the house laden with mature breadfruit. Although the branches touched the corner of the roof, it had shed its load without damaging the roof. The breadfruit formed a neat pile at the back of the house. It was a perfect pile.

All of the breadfruits were picked up and piled into the boot of the car. As we moved from house to house the pastor gave each household a breadfruit. She made sure the members of the church each had a breadfruit. I watched their faces as they received the breadfruit with gratitude as if they had not seen food before. News came over the radio that the airport was inoperative because most of it had been badly damaged. It seemed unlikely that any plane would leave the island for the rest of the week so we were happy to drive around and left the suitcases safely in the home of the missionary and deacon.

We surveyed the land with the pastor. The face of the land was ugly, the sea had reclaimed its course on the main road from Spanish Town to Kingston; fish were swimming about and lamp post and the wires were trailing in the water. Trees, houses and various objects were flattened. I photographed everything I came across and remained close to the walkman, still reporting to my travelling companions. I got really intimate with my walkman in order to drown out the surrounding noise. It brought tears to my eyes to see the devastation caused by the hurricane and to hear over the radio that people were busy looting properties. During the evenings a curfew was introduced in the towns to keep away looters.

On the 15th September we eventually left the island. It was a very close call as we almost missed our flight. We were practically near the airport, some fifteen miles from the home where our luggage was kept when there was a news flash from the airport over the radio, 'All British passengers must check in immediately for departure.' My voice trembled as I shared the news. We all panicked. Pastor Key's abandoned her mission and said to the driver, 'Turn around the car let's get the bags.'

He sped along the road negotiating with the obstacles. At least there was no traffic which made life easier. We got the bags in record time and were on our way to the airport. It was painful to see the damage caused along the once-beautiful flowered decorative stretch of road leading to the airport. The area was now swampy with aeroplanes wrapped around trees. Some were without wings and some had other parts missing. It resembled a battlefield with wounded soldiers. The nearby buildings were lop-sided.

Pianki and I were perhaps the last to check in. The process was made easy by the provision made for disabled passengers. Without delay we boarded the flight with the other passengers and soon the plane lifted and we left the nation behind to clean up the mess. I felt a little guilty when I reflected on the state of the house where we stayed, not much left to eat, the stench and discomfort. The brethren were still there while Pianki and I were escaping.

Our flight to Miami was very comfortable, but we landed too late to make the connecting flight. I feared the worst; that we would have to spend the night in the concourse where some people had clearly slept the previous night. You can imagine my relief and gratitude when the insurance cover made it possible for us to book into a very luxurious hotel for the night, all expenses paid. Provision was made for us to store our bags at the airport. We took a few essentials and as it was too early to check into the hotel, we were able to go and explore down-town Miami. Pianki and I shopped around and had something to eat until it was time to check in.

The hotel was amazing. It was enormous and comfortable. Such opulence! Our room was almost as large as a small one-bedroom flat in the UK. On entering the room, we threw ourselves onto the king size bed. Afterwards we had a much needed bath, followed by room service where we ordered a delicious meal. We finished the evening with a film. My son and I indulged. The following day we were collected for the airport. Although I had had a restful time in the hotel, when I arrived in England I still looked as if I had been washed up on the shore; my Mac was dirty and wrinkled.

The week prior to my leaving the island of Jamaica, Pastor Key contacted the late Overseer G Worldwide Mission Fellowship in England of which I became a member. She had arranged for me to meet with him and to take up membership. Whilst the arrangement was being made, I felt okay and was looking forward to it. I had visited the church on a couple of occasions with Pastor Key before she left for Jamaica. I loved the atmosphere, but it was too far from my home and I felt an obligation to remain with the brethren in the basement who had become my family.

We landed safely in England and Brother Key collected us from Gatwick airport. We stayed at his home and never went to our flat where my adopted son was staying alone. I didn't even bother to phone him. Brother Key arranged for us to visit the overseer the following day. To be truthful I was no longer interested, I felt nervous and fearful. The basement church had lovingly cared for both Pianki and me. They were literally on my door step, two doors away. How could I justify leaving their church to go somewhere else. Yet I felt intimidated by Pastor Key and I also believed God was speaking through her. It was a dilemma.

On the Saturday Dad took me to see overseer G, he was unwell. It was shortly before he died. It was my first time in their home. I looked bedraggled as if I had been belched out of a lion's stomach. Mother G opened the door. I felt she was uncomfortable seeing me which made me even more nervous. I could understand her apprehension if that was the case. I really was not a pretty sight, ravaged by the Gilbert experience. Anyway she showed us into the dining room and went to tell Overseer G. When he entered the room the atmosphere changed. Even though he was a little frail, there was a powerful spiritual presence which enveloped my whole being. It brought back the memory of me meeting with God for the first time in the basement church.

He walked over to me, looked into my eyes and placed his hand on my head, my body quaked and heat moved from my head to my toes. I knew then I was different, still bedraggled, but different. Still Karlene, but different! I believed an impartation had taken place. God through his servant had imparted a special gift, an anointing. Then He spoke, 'Everything will be okay.'

His statement left me wondering, as there was no reason for me to think otherwise. In time I have come to appreciate what he meant. On life's journey, I have held those words foremost in my thought. I now know that God has assured me that every thing will be okay. The statement was in keeping with the scripture that was given to me on several occasions in Jamaica, including at my baptism and when Pastor Key made the arrangement for me to visit the overseer. This verse from the Bible stood out,

"For the mountains shall depart, and the hills be removed; but my kindness shall not depart from thee, neither shall the covenant of my peace be removed, saith the Lord that hath mercy on thee." Isaiah 54:10.

However, I was puzzled by verses 1-4

"Sing O barren, thou that didst not bear; break forth into singing, and cry aloud, thou that didst not travail with child for more are the children of the desolate than the children of the married wife, saith the Lord.

Enlarge the place of thy tent, and let them stretch forth the curtains of thine habitations: spare not, lengthen thy cords, and strengthen thy stakes;

For thou shalt break forth on the right hand and on the left; and thy seed shall inherit the gentiles and make the desolate cities to be inhabited.

Fear not for thou shalt not be ashamed: neither be thou confounded; for thou shalt not be put to shame: for thou shalt forget the shame of thy youth, and shalt not remember the reproach of thy widowhood anymore."

I shared the experience of the storm with the Overseer and told him of the slides I had taken. He asked me to share in the evening service using the slides. I had never done anything like that before but knew I had to do it. He left the room. Mother G, his wife and the mother of the church, who became a special part of my life, seemed much more comfortable. We talked about staying at the Bible school and Pianki going to the local school. At that point I didn't disclose that I had a home in Hackney. We agreed on the details and Pianki and I were taken to see our new room in the Bible School. I thought to myself, this is ridiculous. Here I was battling with mountains of stairs to get to a room with a floor between the room and the kitchen which was in the basement, when I had a much better flat; but the decision was made.

The following day, Sunday, I attended the church. There were about eighty people present. There was an atmosphere of solemnity as we sat and waited. Overseer entered the building, the same presence I experienced the previous day entered with him. It was then that I was totally convinced that I had to be in that church. In the evening I shared the slides of the hurricane with much humour. I was blessed as I ministered to the brethren. It resulted in a collection being made to help Pastor Key to rebuild the church and support the brethren.

Soon after that Sunday, Daddy Key left for Jamaica with the collection. Other members went home to help and support their relatives. Within weeks of the experience the Overseer's health deteriorated and he was admitted to hospital. Then he died. On the day of his funeral I took the most beautiful shot of him lying in the casket. I felt oneness with him as I looked at his face, so still and peaceful, not unlike our first experience, even in death he remained the same.

I settled in the church and became very active. I lived in the Bible school for a short while, it proved to be impractical. The distance to work and back to collect Pianki from school was a challenge. There was no after-school care and it was not possible for Mother G to help every day even though she wanted to. She too loved Pianki, in a special way. So I decided to move back to my home, next to the church in the basement, to people who were a special part of my life. I felt ashamed and ungodly that I had not communicated honestly and clearly what God was doing in my life, but I tried to put it right. Many years later the Pastor's brother expressed his pain when I had taken away Pianki. Even though I was not a member of the church he had much pleasure in visiting us and playing with Pianki.

Chapter 16

There is always better

Five weeks after my return to England I was offered two posts in education. I accepted the one nearer to my home even though it paid less; yet it was much more than what I would have received in Jamaica as head of biological science.

The time spent in Jamaica was immensely beneficial. It left me feeling physically, emotionally and mentally stronger and ready to pursue my career again. However, when I started the job I realised that I was still quite mentally and emotionally delicate. I needed a lot of support to return to an academic life after such a major illness.

Anyway, God must have planned my programme. For the first six weeks in the job, before the Christmas break, all that was required of me was shadowing colleagues, doing research, reading and learning about the organisation and responsibilities of my post. It was called the multicultural centre. Even at that leisurely stroll I struggled with the routine and being focused within the time slots. The discipline of getting up and going to work every day not being able to rest, being around so many different people and attending meetings were all too much; quite stressful. It was at this point that I became aware of why God did not want me to accept the post in Jamaica. It would have made me into a mental wreck.

Anyway, I survived the induction period, learned a lot and was overjoyed when the Christmas break came. I had a good rest and prepared myself to take up my responsibility in January. At the beginning of the term I visited a number of secondary schools who needed support for particular and informal meeting; we ate cucumber sandwiches and drank tea.

The headmistress gave us the background of the school and her teaching experiences. We laughed as she reflected on the fun and challenging times she had had in the school. 'Things have changed dramatically' she said 'since we have become co-educational two years ago I find working with boys much harder, they can be terribly demanding. We were not prepared to meet such dramatic changes'. Before we realised, it was the end of the school day, the bell had rung. It was now too late to meet the staff.

I prayed that I would be placed in that school. God answered my prayer. The management committee agreed that that school met the criteria for support and I would spend a year with them supporting both bilingual and African-Caribbean children in their science lessons. I was delighted. Not only was the school special; two of my favourite colleagues were already working there. The school was informed. The headmistress accepted my placement and was willing to give maximum support. A time was agreed when I would return to meet the staff and organise my timetable.

I started the following week. As well as the support brief I had to develop relevant resources and liase with The Special Needs department. I took a proactive role in the planning and teaching of the science lessons, unlike the norm for Support Teachers from ethnic minority background. Usually they sat next to the identified children and gave one to one support. This marginalized their position as qualified teachers and diminished their status both in the minds of ethnic minority children and the teachers. Often the children did not recognise them as teachers and the mainstream teachers did not involve them in lesson planning.

I managed to negotiate with the teachers in question to co-teach and exchange roles. I led in my specialist area and vice versa. As well as the negative connotation of how support teachers work, I felt that the mainstream teachers were not getting to know the ethnic minority teachers. It was important for the mainstream teachers to become familiar with the needs of those children receiving extra support, so that they could build a positive relationship which was a necessity for when the support ended.

In teaching the classes I gained credibility and respect from both the teachers and pupils. This enhanced my confidence and self-worth which enabled me to integrate readily into the life and culture of the school. I was and informal meeting; we ate cucumber sandwiches and drank tea.

The headmistress gave us the background of the school and her teaching experiences. We laughed as she reflected on the fun and challenging times she had had in the school. 'Things have changed dramatically' she said 'since we have become co-educational two years ago I find working with boys much harder, they can be terribly demanding. We were not prepared to meet such dramatic changes'. Before we realised, it was the end of the school day, the bell had rung. It was now too late to meet the staff.

I prayed that I would be placed in that school. God answered my prayer. The management committee agreed that that school met the criteria for support and I would spend a year with them supporting both bilingual and African-Caribbean children in their science lessons. I was delighted. Not only was the school special; two of my favourite colleagues were already working there. The school was informed. The headmistress accepted my placement and was willing to give maximum support. A time was agreed when I would return to meet the staff and organise my timetable.

I started the following week. As well as the support brief I had to develop relevant resources and liase with The Special Needs department. I took a proactive role in the planning and teaching of the science lessons, unlike the norm for Support Teachers from ethnic minority background. Usually they sat next to the identified children and gave one to one support. This marginalized their position as qualified teachers and diminished their status both in the minds of ethnic minority children and the teachers. Often the children did not recognise them as teachers and the mainstream teachers did not involve them in lesson planning.

I managed to negotiate with the teachers in question to co-teach and exchange roles. I led in my specialist area and vice versa. As well as the negative connotation of how support teachers work, I felt that the mainstream teachers were not getting to know the ethnic minority teachers. It was important for the mainstream teachers to become familiar with the needs of those children receiving extra support, so that they could build a positive relationship which was a necessity for when the support ended.

In teaching the classes I gained credibility and respect from both the teachers and pupils. This enhanced my confidence and self-worth which enabled me to integrate readily into the life and culture of the school. I was included in departmental meetings, training sessions and the social life of the school. I made some good friends. Many children and parents requested to see me. Children often sought me during break and lunch periods to discuss academic, personal and social issues. Eventually, I was asked to be a form teacher. This again was not the norm. I accepted the responsibility which included registration, pastoral, and administrative duties.

As well as my life in the school, I had a life at the multicultural centre. All the support staff from both primary and secondary schools met for in-service training every Friday. It was fun. Although I was enjoying being in school, I missed being in the centre full-time. I had made some good friends there. Not long after I had started at the centre, more staff were appointed, mainly black females, which was not very common in the eighties. We enjoyed friendly chats during break times. I was particularly impressed by one of the appointees. She was always well groomed, dressed in brightly tailored outfits with coordinated head wraps. She moved around briskly, busily doing her job. She always had a radiant countenance, and a good manner with the staff and her reputation of being knowledgeable, creative and sensitive went before her. It was not unusual to hear her infectious giggle as she related to others. Everyone went to her for one reason or another.

At first we shared the same space; desks next to each other in a large room used by other members of staff. Every morning she came into the room and organised her desk placing packed lunch and a snack bar to one corner of it. I would smile as she greeted me but I was not quite sure how to relate to her. I felt a little inadequate and tongue-tied. I often thought, 'What could I say to someone so bright and efficient?'

I eventually started to make a fool of myself by saying silly things and presumptuously partaking of her lunch. Sometimes I deliberately distracted her when it was obvious she was busy. She never got angry with me, she just laughed. At first I wasn't sure what to make of her laughter; but I continued to pester her. When my workload increased in schools I saw less of her. Whenever I was in the centre she was extremely busy. By now I had moved to another space in the office.

Chapter 17

Found a friend

One Friday lunch break I stopped by her desk to say hi. She was just putting on her coat to go home for lunch. She had to collect something. 'Do you want to come home with me?' she asked.

'Okay', I said feeling a little nervous, wondering what we would talk about and why she had invited me home. It was okay to interact with her at work in my silly ways, but somehow I wasn't sure about outside of work. Anyway I accompanied her. She lived in a one-bedroom flat with her partner about five minutes' drive from the centre. When I entered the flat I was taken aback by the décor. There was a lot of black furniture which did not seem to reflect her bright, colourful personality. However, I was soon drawn to the magnificently framed pictures of African images on the wall. I was impressed to know that she and her partner, with whom she owned a framing business, had framed all the pictures.

As I looked around I could see she had a wide selection of music. I cannot remember if she had told me about her music selections or whether I looked at them. But I remember thinking how similar our tastes were, even though as a "Born Again Christian" I now listened primarily to gospel songs and hymns. She showed me to the black armchair which was positioned at the far end of the room under the window ledge asking, 'Would you like some tea?'

'Yes', I said as I flopped into the chair. The seat sank and the floppy arms enclosed part of my body like two giant shoulders. There was a sofa positioned at a right angle from me. She put her handbag in it, leaning it against the arm farther away from where I sat, and then disappeared along the narrow passage to the kitchen, which was to the rear of the flat.

She had not long left when I was distracted from observing the surroundings by the "voice" in my head again. That familiar "voice" which often said what seemed to be ridiculous at times; which told me to do things which seemed impossible and were possibly embarrassing. 'Place your hand on her chest.' I heard.

I muttered to myself, 'Place my hand on her chest?' There was a resounding 'Yes' which jolted me back hard into the armchair, I felt nervous. My temperature must have risen by 300 degrees centigrade. I felt a stream of perspiration running down my chest. I guess my shirt was saturated. 'Why would I want to do such a thing?' I asked myself.

My thoughts wandered to the occasions I had called at her desk and provoked her, even taking bits of her lunch. She never seemed angry, just laughed and promised to bring us more lunch. The command was ridiculous. What would she think of me?

I took in a deep gulp of air, which gave me the courage to respond directly to the "voice". 'Why would I want to touch her chest?' I said. No sooner had I asked the question than she re-entered the room holding two mugs of tea. She came directly to me handing me one of the mugs, which I took. I hoped she hadn't noticed my nervousness. If that were the case it was not obvious, she just turned and sat on the sofa next to her handbag, facing me. I looked across at her, we made eye contact and she started to talk. To be honest I could not distinguish the words she spoke, I just saw her mouth opening and closing. I tried hard to keep my mind focussed on her face in case they wandered to her chest. At that stage I just wanted to leave. Easing myself to the edge of the seat I perched like a young chicken in distress on a dry broken branch.

I was literally burning up with internal heat. Even the seat felt hot. I stretched the mug of tea towards her, 'Let's go.' I said. She looked at her watch and said 'We have sometime yet,' but I kept my hand out-stretched with the tea. She took the mug, ignoring the contents. She didn't even seem angry, just calm and accommodating; with the mugs in her hands she got up from her seat and left for the kitchen. As she did her handbag turned over and the contents poured out onto the seat. Among them was an inhaler. 'Oh no', I thought. That was the reason. God wanted to heal her asthma through me laying my hand on her chest. Through my spiritual walk I have expressed and observed many persons receiving healing when a pastor or someone called by God placed their hand on the sick and prayed. I was devastated. 'Why could I not just trust that "voice"? He has seen me through many situations,' were my thoughts.

I was angry with myself. I had deprived Ankhara of her blessing, I felt guilty, ashamed and embarrassed at the same time. I don't know which was worse refusing to be obedient to that voice which has guided me faithfully so far or realising that I had robbed Ankhara of her healing. We left the flat. I don't believe I said much to her on our way to the centre. I certainly avoided her for the rest of the day and for many days after. From then I felt indebted to her. I knew I had robbed her of her healing.

The friendship between us grew. We enjoyed spending social time together, but I must admit I was always hoping the "voice" would tell me what to do to heal her of the asthma. It still has not happened yet. Ankhara and I often talked and mused about the way in which I was promoted to assistant teacher in charge of one of the two teams in the centre. The voice had spoken and I was obedient. As an outsider looking in, not privy to the voice, Ankhara found the process incredible and it made her curious as to what made me so special that the panel after interviewing those who were short-listed, withheld from making a decision until I was available to be interviewed.

Chapter 18

What's for you, is yours

When we joined the centre a very qualified and experienced member of staff filled the position of acting assistant head of the south team. The organisation had a north and south division. They decided to make the position permanent and it was advertised. It did not occur to me to apply. I felt the acting head was fairly good at the job as she had been acting-up for quite a while. The advertisement was only a formality.

When the post was advertised I was unwell; experiencing difficulties in walking, and continually falling over. My right leg was quite weak. My General Practitioner gave me four weeks' sick leave. On the Friday of the first week I was lying in my bed feeling lonely and helpless, perhaps a little sorry for myself even though the deacon from the church in Jamaica, who was visiting England with Pastor Key, was staying with us for a few days. He was in the living room. Pianki came into my room all ready for school. I don't know why, but I asked him where he would most like to live. To my surprise, he looked at me smiling and said, 'Let's go to Jamaica next Friday.'

I was taken aback. He answered as if he had been waiting for the question. With confidence I assured him that we would go to live in Jamaica next Friday. He left the house for school looking very pleased. I later found out that he had been threatened by the local shop-keeper and he wanted to run away from the area.

I lay on my back looking at the ceiling. As the morning progressed I got restless and kept tossing and turning, moving from one position to the other. Suddenly I felt some water on the side of my neck. I looked up at the ceiling and there it was, water dripping from the flat above. I was furious. I leapt from the bed like a wounded gazelle and hurried along the narrow passage of my flat toward the door. I guess I wanted an outlet for my restlessness. As I reached Pianki's cupboard-sized room the "voice" spoke 'Go and pack your son's clothes, you must take him to Jamaica to Pastor Key and leave him there for a while to be schooled. You must leave next Friday'.

I calmed down as if I had been hypnotised and obediently turned into the room and packed a suitcase with all Pianki's clothes. I then went back into my room and packed my suitcase, after which I got the number of the Strafford Travelling Agency. I reached for the phone with my back to the door. I became aware of someone standing behind. I turned and looked, it was the deacon. His eyes met with the packed suitcases on the floor and he spoke to me in patwa (Jamaica patois) addressing me as 'Ma'. A respectful and endearing phrase used in our church in Jamaica. 'Yu going som whey ma?'

'Mark and I will be with you in Jamaica next Saturday'.

He looked a little puzzled, but nevertheless reached out and grabbed my right hand, which he shook vigorously. 'Very good ma, very good' ma,' he repeated. 'That's wah yu bwoy need.' He then turned and left the room. I was encouraged to make the call. The thought of going to Jamaica caused my blood to "bubble", making me quite hot. I acted spontaneously, giving no thought to the consequences or even the planning, I just acted on impulse. I dialled the number for the travel agency and almost on the first ring there was a voice, 'Hello' Two tickets to Jamaica for next Friday, please' I said. There was a pause.

'We are fully booked' was the sound of the apologetic voice.

'No!' I cried. I held on to the receiver. She stayed with me and searched.

'No,' I refused to accept no and just held the receiver fixed to my ear. I started to feel tense and doubt crept into my mind,

'Perhaps I heard wrong', I thought. I started to recount my steps.

'Saturday?' I asked not so confidently.

'No'

'Sunday?'

'No flights on Sundays.'

Determined again, I returned to Friday. I repeated, 'It is Friday, I know it is Friday.'

It went quiet, but the line was still open, then I heard a masculine voice in the background, 'There are two tickets to Jamaica via Miami.'

'Those are they,' I shouted down the receiver. What a relief! The tickets were booked! I took a deep breath replacing the telephone receiver. I stood in the middle of my room and smiled, then went into the living room beaming, eager to share the good news with the deacon.

'Oh, ma, oh ma', he kept saying.

He was so excited for me. He got up from his seat and grabbed both hands this time and shook them even more vigorously than before. I thought they were going to be dislodged from their sockets. 'That's good ma that's good', he went on to say. At last he let go of my hands and we sat down.

'Will you go and collect the tickets with me on Tuesday on our way back to Pastor Key's home?" I asked.

The deacon and the pastor were going back to Jamaica on the Wednesday. He was so pleased to help. I wondered if he really wanted to collect the tickets to be sure that Pianki and I were really going to be in Jamaica a few days after they were due to return. We collected the tickets. The afternoon when we got to Pastor Key's home I said in a matter of fact way, 'Mom, I will be coming home at the weekend with Pianki to be schooled'.

'Okay' she said, without questioning what I had said.

I was a little surprised that she did not react but just accepted it as if she had been told in advance. Anyway it made me feel comfortable. There was an assurance that God had given us a place in this church family. Pastor Key and I didn't discuss any financial commitment, but I knew that I had a duty to provide for my son and to support the family who would be caring for him.

I returned home to welcome Pianki from school. When I told him all the things that had happened he kept jumping up and down like a jack-in-the-box. I must admit that I also found it hard to contain myself. The day before the flight seemed very long. I was feeling physically and mentally rejuvenated. My legs felt stronger and my thoughts focussed on spending fun times in Jamaica with Pianki and the members of the church. There was a perpetual grin on my face. I was in a state of euphoria and had even forgotten to make travel arrangements to and from the airport. To be honest the thought hadn't surfaced until an old friend who I hadn't heard from for a long time, phoned. 'Hi Sis. Karlene the Lord has placed you on my heart.'

Before he could finish speaking I started my story. Without taking a breath I went through everything we experienced. 'How are you getting to the airport?' he asked. It was then that I realised. With mouth opened wide, I thought 'Oh my God who can I arrange to take us at such short notice?' 'I don't know', I said, sounding a little nervous.

'I will take you' came the voice.

Every minute it was becoming clearer that the trip had been planned by God and His only demand was for me to be obedient. I proceeded to give my friend the details and we arranged the picking-up time.

The Thursday before we departed Mohammed, a co-worker visited me. He brought me an application form for the post that was advertised; assistant head to south team of the organisation. 'Oh, Mohammed, I am not qualified to do that job. Furthermore, the acting assistant-head is more than capable. She has been doing it for a long time. I cannot see anyone else getting it.' But Mohammed kept pressing for me to apply. He seemed confident in my abilities and favoured me to get the job. I must admit I was a little surprisedMohammed and the assistant were from the same racial background - Asian. They seemed to get on well and in my experience in the UK, Asians are generally supportive of each other. To be honest I was more focused on the trip to Jamaica. Mohammed kept pressing.
'You must apply; you are the one for this job'.
I just smiled and reiterated, 'The acting assistant-head has the job in the bag'. I was convinced that no one else would get the job, even if they were equally or more qualified and experienced.

The Head of the team was also an Asian gentleman; he worked extremely well with the acting head. There was no need for change. There was nothing I could say to deter Hammed, he was insistent and would not listen to me until I did something about the application form. For peace sake I took the form. I looked at it, 'Gosh', I thought, 'how am I going to get my head around these questions?' Anyway I went through and filled in what I could, leaving sections incomplete including names of appropriate referees. I returned the form to him apologising for not putting it into an envelope. That did not seem to matter to him. He held the completed form like a treasured gift. It was then that he asked about my health. I told him about my trip and he listened without making any comment. After that he updated me on what had been going on in the centre. I was pleased that he visited but all I wanted to do was to organise ourselves for the early morning travel; what to wear and eat.

The following day Pianki and I left for Jamaica. The flight was via Miami. I was grateful for the arrangement of the wheelchair service at the airport. It was heavenly, not having to walk what seemed to be a never-ending journey from the check-in point to boarding, especially when I would need to keep up with the pace of my energetic son.

In the United Kingdom we were privileged to ride on the airport buggy. Pianki loved the ride. In Miami this was not the case, they used the wheelchair but he had to walk. Pianki got into all sorts of mischief, weaving in and out of people along the concourse. He complained that it was not fair that he should be walking. The people were generally accommodating, some laughed and others played with him. He appeared to have attracted the attention of everyone, engaging them into conversation. I felt really stressed trying to anticipate his next trick and hoping he would not upset anyone. Finally, we arrived at the departure lounge where we were left to wait for the connecting flight to Jamaica.

I sat in the wheelchair feeling totally exhausted, counting every second to the next flight whilst Pianki continued to race about. I willed the time to pass quicker, but it felt slow. At last I heard, 'Wheelchair passengers and families with young children to board first'. We fitted both categories. The porter returned to help us on to the plane. It was comforting to be seated and settled in the plane before the rest of the passengers were allowed on. We sat and watched as the tired-faced passengers came on loaded with bags on their shoulders and in their hands. Some struggled to secure their luggage in the over head cabins. The plane was full and ready to depart.

The flight from Miami to Jamaica was incredibly short. No sooner had the aeroplane ascended and settled at an altitude than it started to descend. It felt like a roller coaster ride, even though I have never had that experience. Anyway I was glad to be home again in Jamaica. As the porter wheeled me into the open air from the plane and into the building which was as hot as outside even though the ceiling fans where rotating at a rapid speed, the heat penetrated my body. I arose from my sitting position, which had become slumped since leaving in the cold, to being upright.

I looked ahead along the long corridor feeling a little uncomfortable as the porter pushed over the series of sleeping policemen that were placed at regular intervals. At the end of the passage we made a right turn and then a left into an open space where passengers were queuing to go through immigration. I was pushed to the front and came to a standstill behind a white line whilst the immigration officer finished with a passenger. He was seated quite high in a cabin; the upper part was surrounded with glass so we could see from his head to his chest. There was a slit in the glass through which documents were passed.
'Next', came the deep, but tired voice. The porter wheeled me forward, Pianki followed. The officer took my papers. 'Only one passport,' I heard.

It was then that I realised that Pianki and I were travelling on the same passport. I was not sure how that would work with him coming to stay in a country without a passport. From the wheelchair I craned my neck to look up at the officer as he looked down from the cage. 'Pianki, Pianki, A wha kin a name this ya,' came the abrupt cross voice. I froze and looked directly into his eyes. 'So you de mother?' he asked.

'Yes' I replied

'An de father from,'

'St. Kitts' I said. He pressed his head against the fibre-glassed window to get a clearer look at us. His expression was fierce and cold. Pianki held on to the back of the wheelchair.

'How long yu intend to stay on di island?'

'Two weeks' I said

'Teck im out a di country in two weeks' he retorted, as he wrote something in the passport. Then he hammered the page with the stamp and passed back the passport to the porter who handed it me. When I looked on the stamped page he had written 'remove the said child from this country in two weeks'. I felt unease, possibly numb. I was impatient to get outside to tell Pastor Key what had transpired.

The rest of the clearance was smooth. We were the first passengers to get out. The walkway to the open space was thronged with staring eyes. My eyes scanned the faces as the porter pushed me along. Suddenly they met with those of Pastor Key's. A broad grin spread across her face and her lips moved up and down. Pianki had not seen her, he was still recovering from the flight. She turned back into the crowd. Within seconds she and the deacon were at the bottom of the walkway. Pianki saw them and rushed toward them. For a moment I forgot the incident with the immigration officer. I got out of the wheelchair and we hugged. It was all so exciting. The deacon went to collect the car. Whilst waiting everything came back and I told her what had happened. 'Yu believe God spoke to you,' she said

'Yes, mom,' I said.

Taking my hands into hers she prayed, thanking God for his instructions, direction and guidance in my life. As she finished praying Deacon came alongside to collect the baggage to put into the car which was parked a few feet away at the pick-up point. We all loaded in the car. Pianki and I sat in the back and we headed for the long journey to Pastor Key's home. The first part of the journey was along the sea. As we drove the cool breeze blew over my face. I sat peacefully, trying to comprehend all that had happened. Here I was in Jamaica, all because that "voice", that familiar "voice" which had become my trusted guide, teacher and friend had spoken to me clearly and unequivocally. I should have been in my bed in England, but the "voice" overrode everything. As we moved away from the sea into the city the atmosphere got hotter and hotter. It was not long before I was fast asleep. I was woken by the noise around me. 'Yes', we had arrived. The gates to Pastor Key's home were opened and the car slowly cruised along the side of the house next to a doorway which led into the passage of the house.

By now it was quite dark. We all got out of the car. Pastor Key's daughter opened the door to the passage and we went into the house. Pianki and I were shown to the first room which had become ours. There was that familiar fresh smell of lemon. The double bed was covered with matching pastel shaded bed linen. I sat at the foot of the bed and removed my shoes. Deacon Sam put all our baggage into the room and Pastor Key encouraged us to rest until the morning. I didn't need to be persuaded. Soon Pianki and I had snuggled up under the sheet, fast asleep.

The bright sunrays streaming in through glass louvres and the cluttering noise of pots in the kitchen not far from our bedroom disturbed my rest. I rose form the bed and stretched, walked to the window opened the louvres letting in more fresh air, and looked outside. It was dry and bright. There was a fence punctuated by trees which separated Pastor Key's yard from the plot of land next door. It was well cultivated with green and luscious plants at different stages of development. The leaves arranged themselves creatively to receive their fair share of light. The banana shrubs seemed to have created an umbrella over the smaller plants but the tear in their fronds allowed light through. Growing from the head of the banana plants where the leaves clustered was solid stalk with bunches of green meagre bananas bursting through. Some were still enclosed in a red casing with white petals dangling from the emaciated fingers of bananas. Others were at different stages of maturity where the bananas were arranged in hands of five to nine on the stalk.

There were other fruit trees with young fruits hanging from thread-like structures attached to the branches. To get a closer look at the amazing beauty and creation of nature, I donned my dressing gown and slippers and went outside after first calling at the bathroom. I stepped down from the passage into the yard, stood on the step for a few seconds and gasped deep gulps of air, it was warm and fresh, and my lungs heaved forward and upward as if to say, 'I really needed that'.

The experience made my legs feel stronger. A thought of being from the amphibian species which meant that I needed warmth to maximise my movement, made me smile. I took slow steps toward the fence and went and stood next to a lime tree. It was full of brilliant blossoms. A few feet away were two tall towering coconut trees ladened with well-formed green jelly coconuts in clusters and shielded by some giant rustic brown and yellow fronds. Such a contrast with the much shorter lime trees with their branches spreading out and covered with small pear-shaped oily looking leaves. Between the trees were beds of flowering plants. What a medley of colours.

At the gate there was an enormous mango tree with a giant trunk and long leaves with protruding veins. The leaves obscured the view to the right side of the house, which faced the main road. Whilst standing in the yard the road got very busy with the morning traffic, cars whizzing to and fro stirring up a lot of dust. Suddenly the air was not so clear, but it had not detracted from the beauty of the surrounding plants. From where I stood I could see across the road to the left into the far distance where there were many detached houses. Opposite Pastor Key's was a playing field, to the right of which was a small grocery shop, partially visible. I stood and stared, trying to understand all that had happened over the last few days.

I jumped when the strong, deep voice of Pastor Key said, 'Miss Karlene yu cum home,' I turned and looked in her direction as she stepped from the passage into the yard with a beam on her face. I could hear Pianki chatting away inside. Pastor Key came closer to me pointing out the places around, giving their history. We were interrupted by a gentle voice coming from the door, Pastor Key's daughter.

'Mom, breakfast is ready'. My eyes met with hers and she grinned. I smiled back.

Mom looked at her and said, 'Morning Arge, Masta Pianki has come home to go to school.'

'I know Mom,' she said stepping into the yard.

The loosely fitting flip-flops made a clicking noise whilst she walked toward us. Audrey joined us and we stood for a few minutes talking before going inside. We went into the very large lounge-dining room and sat around the table which was decked with various cooked dishes, plates, cups and utensils; in fact, all the trimmings.

Breakfast was fun. There was lots of laughter as Mom held our attention with stories and folk tales. Pianki ate and actively enjoyed the stories, asking questions. At times my mind wandered to the practicality of the care for Pianki once I returned home, after all both Mom and Audrey had busy lives; Mom in the ministry, and Audrey as a full time primary school teacher. I consoled myself by holding onto the promise from God which said that He will provide. I believed that he had arranged for us to be there and would provide for us to stay. The jokes continued.

Chapter 19

Home coming

On the Sunday we all went to church which was over ten miles away. It was my first visit to the new concrete structure which replaced the board building that had been demolished by Hurricane Gilbert in 1988. Everyone greeted me, some hugged, and others shook my hand while others looked, nodded and smiled. The service was like a celebration of our homecoming. Mom made Pianki and I feel very special. We were asked to address the congregation. I shared my testimony and Pianki spoke confidently about being pleased to be in Jamaica. After the morning service we had lunch, the adults sat around the church yard and chatted, the children played. Pianki was in his element. The day was full without an opportunity to rest so by the time we were ready to return home I was very tired and I fell asleep in the car.

We woke early Monday morning, congregated in the lounge where we prayed and read from the Bible and Mom explained the scripture. It lasted for about an hour, after which she suggested that we should get ready to go and register Pianki at Glenmuir preparatory School, a feeder school to the Glenmuir High school. Both were rated as the best schools in the parish and Glenmuir High as one of the top schools on the island. Many of the islands' leading politicians, professionals and sport successes had attended the school. In fact, the then minister of finance, for Jamaica, was a former student.

The school was really quite close to Mom's home and it would not be difficult for Pianki to get to and from it. To my amazement a journey that should have taken us a few minutes' walk after a five minutes' ride in a taxi to the gates, seemed endless. We alighted from the taxi either before or after the school and kept walking around in circles, in and out of avenues and closes. At last a school appeared before us. It was on a slight gradient. It seemed to have appeared out of nowhere. I was relieved. I did not think I could have endured another step. We went through the gates, into the yard and up some steps at the front of the building which led us into a small reception area. A tall, slim lady with hair closely cut to the scalp, possibly in her early forties welcomed us. 'Hello, can I help you?' Her face glowed with health. There was a slight accent, she was not Jamaican. Mom spoke explaining the situation. The lady smiled.

'This is Thomas Moore Preparatory'.

Imagine we had passed the sign outside without realising that we were at the wrong school. It really did not matter to me at that moment. I just wanted to rest. Mom looked shocked. She prided herself on knowing the island very well and her parish like the back of her hand. To get lost in one's own parish was unheard of for her.

Mom asked to see the head teacher. Again the lady smiled, this time she chuckled a little. Extending her hand to Mom she said, 'Mrs. Wilson, the Head'. We all laughed. After shaking hands, Mrs Wilson led us into a room to the side of the reception area. We were shown to some seats. I literally flopped into one of them; my legs could no longer support my weary body. Mrs Wilson went and sat behind her desk. In the background we could hear a chorus of poems and timetables being repeated by the children in their classes.

Mrs Wilson presented the background to the school, a catholic preparatory that accepts workers from overseas. Mrs Wilson was on placement from one of the African states. She looked at us and said, 'There is only one available place in the school and it's for a grade three pupil, the year above Pianki's age. But I will give Pianki a mathematics test. 'If he is successful he can start tomorrow.' My heart missed a beat. I knew Pianki's English was quite good, he read extensively and enjoyed writing and listening to stories but he was lazy regarding Mathematics.

Mrs Wilson took the test paper from one of her drawers, moved to a small desk that was in the corner of the room and invited Pianki to sit at it. He sat comfortably and started to read the paper. I sat at the edge of my seat feeling tense. Within a short time Pianki completed the test, dealing with the mathematical problems as if he had rehearsed them. He looked at me and smiled, it made me more nervous. Pianki handed the paper to

Mrs. Wilson. All eyes were on her as she marked the paper. One tick after another, as my eyes followed her hand down the page, only one x mark. The smile on my face broadened, my shoulders went back and I slid back into the chair.

'Well done, Pianki you only had one wrong'. She turned to us and said, 'Pianki can start tomorrow but you need to bring in his medical record. It is a prerequisite to entrance into schools in Jamaica.' Again, my heart throbbed. This was another indicator that I had not planned the trip.

'I have not brought his papers, Mrs Wilson. I was led by the Lord to make the trip.' I said.

Mrs Wilson said, 'I will make an exception in this case provided the papers are sent as soon as you return to England.' We were about to sort out the details when a lady even taller than Mrs. Wilson filled the doorway, blocking the light. All eyes turned towards her. She had a pile of used books sandwiched between her hands. After greeting us she looked at Mrs Wilson and said,

'Mrs Wilson, one of the pupils from last year's class 3 would like to get a buyer for these books.'

Mrs Wilson smiled and looked at us. We smiled back. 'You can give those to Miss Rickard for Pianki. He will be joining us tomorrow.'

We took the books and paid for them. I promised to send the medical card once I returned to England. We got all the details and went off to the stores to get Pianki's uniform and equipment. Mrs. Wilson had given him permission to wear his trainers for a few weeks but everything else had to be in place. I was able to pay for all the necessities and to give Mom some money for his shoes, taxi fare to and from school, food and other essentials for a period of time until I could send some more from the United Kingdom. She took me to the bank to open an account. For the rest of the week and the first four days of the following week I took Pianki to school in the mornings and collected him in the evenings.

Chapter 20

The pain of separation

On the Friday of the second week, it was time for me to return to England. Mom and Pianki accompanied me to the airport. I tried hard not to think of the inevitable, me leaving my son behind. I kept talking to everyone in the car. As we drew near the airport my heart started to race. Occasionally I looked at Pianki sitting next to me and forced a smile. I wanted to undo all I had done. The reality of what had happened dawned on me. 'If only Pianki would cry and refuse to stay, I could take him back' but he sat quietly in the car.

Within a short period of time I was being taken through the barrier in the wheelchair. Pianki stood still next to pastor and stared. I stole a quick glance at him being careful to avoid eye contact. I felt when my right leg stiffened. 'What had I done?' I thought. I wanted my son back. I was going to leave him six thousand miles away with these people. They no longer felt like a family. I was questioning myself. How much do I really know about them? I now felt they were strangers. 'Please, God let him run after me'. I urged. But Pianki stood transfixed and stared.

Whilst I was checking in I could not see him. But Pianki was visible again when the porter wheeled me along the concourse enclosed by large sheets of glass separating the passengers from their well-wishers. Mom must have taken him into the small gift shop as he now had a magazine in his hand. As I passed he moved closer to the glass, which separated us. With his forehead almost pressing onto it, he kept his eyes focussed on the magazine, which he held to one side. I looked back from the wheelchair until they were no longer in sight, or rather I was out of sight.

I was now going through the immigration barrier; the wheelchair porter took my passport and handed it to the officer who was perched on his high chair behind a tall narrow desk. Looking at the passport carefully, I wanted him to notice where he had stamped it, but he just looked down at me and handed back the passport. Not a word was said. I looked intensely in his face as the porter pushed me along. I was sure it was the same officer. 'How could he not notice the stamp prohibiting my son from staying and allow me to go through,' I thought.

Suddenly I felt the tears running down my face, my stomach kept churning and I wanted to get out of the wheelchair and run back for my boy, my only son. I felt so weak. I went through various security checks to which I was oblivious. It was little wonder that I remembered to collect my personal belongings after they were checked. The porter pushed me into the departure lounge and left me parked near the toilets as I waited for the plane. There I sat and cried unconcerned. Normally I would be impatiently checking and monitoring the time for the next plane.

I recollected the first sermon I heard in the basement church in England where I had met the pastor. It was about Abraham who had given up his son to God as a sacrifice, but God stepped in at the appointed time and provided an animal sacrifice. That sermon had disturbed my spirit so much. I kept saying, 'Please Lord never let that happen to me, I couldn't give away my only son.' Here I was doing the very thing I dreaded, at least that is how it felt. 'Who is to say I would ever live to see him again'.

I gripped my abdomen as the pain stabbed like an active embryo kicking through the lining of my womb. I was in utter despair. The more I thought the more the tears ran down my face. Suddenly, there was a debate going on in my head as to why he had not asked for Pianki. I resolved the contention by saying, 'God must have blinded his eye', which relates to a Bible story where God allowed an incident to take place in front of an audience who could not see what was happening. By now the stabbing had intensified, which made the rest of my body physically weak. I guessed my face was covered with watermarks from the tears. I really wanted to scream.

I cannot recollect getting onto the plane, but I knew I was in Miami. The ground staff mostly Mexican and white Americans, who remembered us on the outbound journey were asking for the little boy. At first I would say, 'I left him in Jamaica'. They would look at me with disdain and outrage as if to say,

'How could you be so wicked'?

One woman even said 'How could you? Such a nice boy.' That made me feel wretched, callous and heartless. I felt physically sick like vomiting. 'Why, why', I muttered like a demented fool. Why did I do it, would I ever see him again?' I cried even more. I could hardly see through the water rushing from my eyes. To avoid being questioned anymore I sat and buried my head into my hands desperately willing the plane to arrive. The wait felt heavy and long, I thought it would never come to an end. When I heard, 'Wheelchair passengers and parents with young children to board first' I almost jumped for joy, my only moment of victory since leaving Pianki behind.

Once on the plane I felt more relaxed but continued to cry. I was placed in the aisle seat. As we were taxiing along the runway I realised that the woman in the middle to my left and the man across the aisle to the right, were together. I felt they desperately wanted to sit next to each other. I could feel their eyes burning into my cheeks but I ignored them. Perhaps, if they had asked I would have moved, but I wasn't going to be the Miss nice lady. I had just lost my child and I was grieving. Who cared if they were unhappy? After all they could see and speak to each other. I was alone and my pain was more important than their pleasure. I just sat and cried and cried until I was in England. I cannot remember sleeping or eating on the journey. I knew I was being driven on the airport buggy totally exhausted, to check out and collect my luggage. My mind drifted again and I was home. The young man who took us to the airport was bringing my cases into the lounge. There were lots of letters piled up behind the door on the floor. I stooped to gather them. He went and I was left alone.

Looking around at the pictures on the wall I wondered what Pianki was doing. Slowly I sat on the settee and stared into space for a few seconds before opening the letters. Most of them were junk mail. I came across a response to the job application I made when I was leaving for Jamaica. My heart missed a beat, they had asked me to an interview the previous Tuesday whilst I was in Jamaica, 'So near and yet so far.' was my thought. To have had that job suddenly seemed very important. The additional income would have been helpful to pay for my fare to visit Pianki during his school holidays.

I was angry at myself for not being more serious about applying for the job when I heard a noise at the door, the letters for the day had arrived. I went and picked them up. To my amazement there was another letter from the centre, they asked me to attend an interview for the same job on the Monday. I looked intently at the letter and kept re-reading to make sure that I was not mistaken. To my knowledge once an applicant failed to respond to an interview offer he/she would be eliminated. It provided a distraction from the negative thoughts of having left Pianki in Jamaica. I tried to conceptualise what it would be like to do the job. I even began to convince myself that I would be the best person. I was motivated by the additional income. I pondered over the letter and the possibility of getting the job until I was too tired to think anymore, then I went to sleep.

Chapter 21

Can it get better?

I slept until quite late into the following day, Sunday morning. In fact, I was woken by the doorbell. Not feeling very sociable I almost ignored it but something propelled me to open the door. 'Max, what are you doing here?' I shouted. I stood and stared at his tall figure slightly stooped with a bag hanging from his right shoulder. He was an old friend, but I had not seen or heard from him for many years. He reached down and hugged me. It felt good, I wanted it to last for ever. I needed to feel loved after battering myself for leaving Pianki. As I disentangled myself from his grip I took his arm and led him into the kitchen where we sat around the table. Max didn't have to ask me how I was. No sooner had he sat down and rested his bag on the table than I bombarded him with all the events of the last two weeks.

Max had successfully prepared many candidates for job interviews. 'Get a pen and paper and let's get ready for that interview tomorrow' he said as he smiled at me. I responded immediately. Max read the job specification, thought about the questions and started to talk. He was like an open faucet. I felt overwhelmed and couldn't keep up with what he was saying. 'Max, Max, I can't keep up, can I tape what you are saying'

'Of course', he said. I went for my faithful tape recorder, placed it next to him and turned it on. Max started again. Guided by the specifications he addressed each point. I tried to focus on his every word but it was a struggle to keep up. Anyway I managed to ask some questions and talked through certain issues. I tried my best, but being overwhelmed by tiredness I started to nod. 'Karlene, I will just finish off addressing the question and then go, you are still tired from the flight.' I was grateful for his consideration. He rose from the table, took his bag and left. I took the tape and went to my bedroom intending to rest before listening to it. To my surprise I listened twice before falling asleep. After that I never surfaced until early Monday morning.

I woke feeling refreshed, and got dressed. There was ample time to listen to the tape and make some notes. I got the tape recorder ready and sat on the edge of my bed, but instead of playing the prepared tape for the interview, I replaced it with a tape of old gospel songs which I had borrowed from the friend who took us to the airport. I sat comfortably on the bed rocking to the rhythm, enjoying myself. Seeing me you would never have thought that I was about to go to an interview within the next two hours. I was interrupted by the "voice", 'Read Jeremiah 1:5, 8 and 17.'
"Before I formed thee in the belly I knew thee;
And before thou camest forth out of the womb
I sanctified thee, and I ordained thee a prophet
unto the nations".
Be not afraid of their faces: for I am with thee to
deliver thee, saith the Lord.
Thou therefore gird up thy loins, and arise, and
speak unto them all that I command thee:
be not dismayed at their faces, lest I confound
thee before them."
I reread the passage several times. Particular words became fixed in my mind. 'Before you were born I knew you', 'I will confound thee', 'Be not afraid of their faces'.

I wondered what the message was about. I felt a little nervous, which increased when I noticed that it was time to leave for the interview and I had not listened to the tape once. I jumped to my feet, picked up the prepared prompt cards, put them into my handbag, and donned my coat. This was done in one quick swoop.

The journey was short. I parked next to the building and entered the main entrance which led into a large square hall. Around the hall there were several doors leading into offices and the library. The main office was opposite to the entrance. On that particular day it was difficult to see the doors once in the hall as they were obscured by display boards. I walked along the passage created by the display boards toward the main office. I was several feet away when Cathy, the secretary emerged to greet me. She was warm and friendly which helped me to relax. Cathy showed me to a chair placed next to the room in which I would be interviewed.

'Would you like a cup of tea?'
'Yes, please' I said, placing my belongings on the floor.

She must have had it already prepared because within minutes she handed me the cup of tea. Everything was happening very quickly. I carefully placed the tea on the floor and fished the cards from my bag. Before I could get comfortable the door opened and my boss stood in the space, 'Come in Miss Rickard'. I fumbled with my belongings, leaving the tea behind. My heart really started to race again. 'Gosh,' I thought on entering the room. In front of me were three pairs of eyes staring, waiting for me to be seated and my boss to join them.

'Please sit down,' I heard.

I was more than willing to obey. Another moment standing and I would have been in a heap on the floor - my legs were getting weak. I sat. My boss joined the panel. Then there were four pairs of eyes penetrating through me, some even smiled. My immediate thought was to get up and run. Then the "voice" spoke, repeating a section that I had read earlier in the Bible, 'Look them in their eyes and be not afraid. I will confound thee'. The word 'confound' played on my mind. The thought of being confounded by God was scary. I was desperate for a solution. Somehow I found one, the next thing I knew I was groping in my bag for my glasses. I needed them for reading. With sweaty palms I removed them from the case and put them on. Suddenly, I became confident, sat upright and looking at the panel, the faces before me were mottled and out of focus. For a moment I wanted to laugh aloud. I could no longer see those distinctively scary eyes.

The questions started. One followed another. I opened my mouth and the answers flowed. I gave no thought to the questions, just responded. There were times when my words sounded like direct quotes from the Bible. I felt relaxed. Then I heard 'Thank you Miss Rickard, would you like to ask any questions?' I looked at my watch. Fifty minutes had passed; I was now feeling exhausted, devoid of energy. I dropped my shoulders, took off my glasses and looked at the panel.

'I am tired can I go home?' They glanced at each other. At that point one of the panellists read out the terms and conditions of the job, most of which went into space.

My boss came from her seated position to escort me to the door, all very formal. I could barely get up from the seat. My legs were wobbling. She walked me to the main door of the building, seeing me to my car. 'We will be in touch soon,' she said as I went through the door. My main concern was to rest. I got into the car, positioned myself and sat for a while. My mind went blank for a moment. 'It was over,' I thought. Slowly I left the car park and made my way home. I drove very slowly. I had not long got through the door when the phone rang. It was Joyce, my boss. 'Who is your referee?' she asked.

'Candy from Leytonstone Secondary School,' was my response. It was then I remembered how incomplete the application was. I put down the receiver and relaxed on the settee. The phone rang again. It was Joyce. 'We would like to offer you the position.' I was caught off guard. I didn't expect the decision to have been made so quickly. I went quiet. I felt terrified. All my confidence went through the door. I was no longer sure of my ability to do the job.

I wanted to say, 'Thanks, but no thanks'. I was about to turn down the offer when the "voice" kicked in. I knew I had to say yes. 'Thank you', I blurted out, putting down the receiver. I rested well that day.

The promotion was almost equal in status and much better paid than the job God told me not to accept in Jamaica. Besides, I had developed personally and professionally in working as a support teacher for the organisation. I was in a much more stable position to cope with the demands of the job. The major responsibility of the job was to negotiate placement for the support staff for children with special educational needs in the secondary schools south of the borough. Among support staff was the acting assistant head. I had anticipated that supervising her would be challenging but I had under-estimated the extent.

The day I had to review her placement, I prayed that God would give me wisdom and insight to manage. We arranged the time and location and I entered the school. The office staff were friendly and efficient. They notified her. I was asked to make my way up to her room. At that point I felt uncomfortable. I walked along the long corridor towards her room hoping that when I got there everything would be perfect. I knocked on the door, 'Come in,' said a voice. She had positioned herself around the table and all the necessary documents were laid out on the table. I smiled at her and sat on the chair made available.

'Hello, how are you?' I said. Before I could say anything else she stood up abruptly with tears in her eyes, looked at me and said,
'I can't do this.' She took her handbag and left the room. I sat and

stared into space. I was numb with embarrassment.

The second round was worse. It was at our team meeting. She asked difficult questions to unnerve me and had a meeting within the main meeting. I struggled to keep to the agenda, chairing ineffectively. Her strategy was to denigrate my work, but God granted me favour. There were a couple of experienced staff members who recognized what was happening and steered the meeting in the right direction. I managed to keep my head, cover all the key issues and close on time. I came out of the meeting more aware of how to manage a meeting. I felt stronger but disappointed that we were not able to resolve our differences in private.

The following week I had to repeat the review. I prepared myself by praying and asking God to perform a miracle. I believed He spoke into my mind to buy a Christian card expressing my sympathy, understanding and love. On that occasion everything went according to plan, the review was done professionally. The following day I saw her in the centre. We greeted each other, I smiled and handed her the card. She accepted saying, 'Thank you'.

About a week later she approached me. 'Thank you for the card, I was brought up in a Christian home and my parents are Christians but I drifted. Right now my mother is not well, could you pray for her?' It was like a breath of fresh air to my ears. I smiled to myself. From then on with God's help I was always well prepared for meetings. I prayed before-hand and ensured I did my home-work on items listed for discussion. With every meeting I improved.

Chapter 22

Yet another miracle

After I left Pianki in Jamaica without a passport Mom arranged an appointment with an immigration officer to get him a student visa. On the day in question, I phoned to find out the outcome. The phone rang once and Mom was at the other end tripping over her every word with excitement. 'K, Pianki has been given a student's permit, the officer prayed that you will be home soon as well, Isn't God good?' I sat with the receiver stuck to my ear, a smile lit up my face as I listened to all she had to say. I didn't say much. Within a couple of months the application that I had made for the teachers' exchange programme was approved. It was indeed a miracle.

A prerequisite for the programme was to be in good health. I was far from that. Bleeding from my womb constantly, the gynaecological unit had arranged for me to have a hysterectomy. Whilst I was having a medical the nurses discovered an enormous sore on my back. The flesh had been eaten away to the extent of almost exposing my spine. One nurse discovered it, but soon I was swarmed by several nurses. The painful expressions on their faces as they gathered around made me want to scream. They discussed amongst themselves, bombarding me with questions that I could not answer. Swabs were taken and I was eventually told to wait in the examination room for a specialist. It seemed forever. I was afraid of the unknown. 'How could I have developed such a dreadful sore on my back,' I thought.

Eventually two doctors, one wearing a suit and the other a white overcoat, came into the room. They started the questions again. So many questions, I felt I was facing the Spanish Inquisition. 'I don't know; I don't know' was my repeated response. 'How can I answer your questions, I only became aware of the problem at the same time as the nurses'. I was not in pain; but as they prodded it I was being stifled by the foul smell of rotten flesh.

After much pondering and reasoning they concluded that I had burnt myself. Their story was that I sat close to a radiator with lots of clothing. Due to the poor sensitivity of my skin and impaired nerve endings I did not feel when I was being burnt. Then the consultant said, 'Miss Rickard I will arrange an appointment for you to have that wound grafted'. He turned to the other doctor and said, 'The wound needs to be cleaned, a piece of skin can be removed from her right leg and grafted on to her back.' I was horrified. They talked across me as if I were not there or just an animal to be treated. They took a swab and left me to get dressed. The appointment was made for the skin graft.

On the day of the appointment the result from the swab had not yet returned from the lab. As I sat and waited for them to locate the results I heard the "voice", that familiar "voice". 'Refuse the operation.' I shuddered.
'What will I say to these experts, where will I get the courage and confidence to go against their medical advice?' The wait became heavy and frustrating. I got extremely anxious. Eventually I went to the receptionist and asked to see the doctor. 'I will not be taking the operation.' I said. He looked surprised. He proceeded to explain why it had to be done, but I was unmoved. He stared into my face, his eyes were still and he was going slightly red. He left the room and returned some minutes later accompanied by another doctor. They kept saying, 'You must have this operation if not …..' My ears went deaf to the lengthy explanation. 'Miss Rickard why don't you want this operation' I heard. I looked at him stunned. 'I don't want to do it. It will be dangerous; I know it will.'

They looked at each other and left the room. Next a feisty female surgeon, possibly in her late thirties early forties, came in. She was a tyrant, rude and unprofessional. She looked at me intently and allowed the plethora of threats to spew from her pouting lips. I ignored her. She left and sent in an African male doctor to plead to my ethnicity. 'What have you done?' he asked. He sounded pathetic.

'I don't know' was my response in a matter of fact way.
'You have burnt yourself,'
'So you are telling me, I really don't know, I cannot recall what happened, but I won't have any operation.'

He too turned and went away. I expected the firing squad. But he came back with a white colleague.

I was getting really fed up. I sat up straight, with a blank stare into their faces. They left, telling me to get dressed. Finally, the consultant came to see me. 'Miss Rickard as you will not have the operation I will arrange for your GP, to have the wound dressed daily.' There was not much they could have done since I had refused the operation. Eventually, they gave up, but they were furious. Before I left the hospital, I sat and waited for a letter to be typed to my GP so that the wound could be treated. The technician turned up with the result of the swab. It showed that the wound was infected with a particular fungus and if the skin from the right leg had been grafted onto the back, it would have fallen off and caused scarring.

On the basis of the results it was agreed for me to have the wound dressed daily at the local clinic using a specified dressing. Every day I went faithfully to the clinic for a fresh dressing. The stench was unbearable but gradually it got better. One day my General Practitioner looked at me and said that the trip to Jamaica would be good. I was quite surprised as the wound had not completely healed and furthermore the gynaecologist had recommended hysterectomy to stem the constant profuse bleeding. Nonetheless my doctor signed the application form giving medical clearance to leave the country on the exchange programme within the next three months. I believe God had spoken to him.

The process for the exchange began. I attended all the relevant meetings and left for Jamaica with a team of four. I was about to work in Jamaica on a British salary. I was in the position to provide additional financial support for Pianki and the church as well as spending more time with him. The exchange was with Ms Bogle, the great granddaughter of one of Jamaica's national heroes, Paul Bogle from Morant Bay in the parish of St. Thomas.

Whilst on the island the problem with my womb persisted. An appointment was made to see a gynaecologist. A strange thing happened at the clinic, I was asked to see a specialist who focussed on my chest and examined my armpit, I thought that they must have made a mistake, but decided to continue with the examination. 'Have you ever noticed any lump under your arm?' 'No,' I said. The look on her face made me wonder if she going to say something sinister. She pressed harder into the armpit. 'There is quite a large lump formed in your gland, I want you to go to the Barbican hospital to be tested for Tuberculosis (TB), I will give you a letter'. I sat dumbstruck. She continued, 'Have you ever been tested for T.B?'

'Yes, but the result was negative.'

That took me back to when I was tested, the site was slightly raised but they decided it was negative. However, to be certain, the test needed to be repeated within a few years. It never happened. The thought of a positive result made me anxious; not to mention the lump under my arm. My grandmother had died of sebaceous cancer.

After the examination I went back to the waiting room to join Mom. I handed her the letter and told her what had happened. She took it in her stride and calmly said, 'We will go now as we are not very far.' Deacon Sam took us to the hospital. It was an old unfriendly building needing repairs and possibly some modern equipment. Inside was overcrowded every space occupied, even sections of the corridor were being used. Mom and I walked the length of a long corridor to the T.B. unit. It felt like a death march.

When we arrived, I was invited to sit in a part of the corridor whilst the Heaf test was prepared. The nurse was friendly. 'Roll up your right sleeve Karlene please, nothing to be afraid of.' She stamped the lower part of my arm with a small instrument. It left a small circular imprint with about five tiny dots. It was quick and painless. I didn't have to wait long before an enormous lump which looked like a blister grew where she had stamped the dot. With every minute it grew bigger and bigger. I thought it would never stop. It was evident that the result was positive and I had T.B. I was afraid, not sure what it would mean. For the first time Mom looked concerned. That did not help my case. She asked me to cover the raised area with my long sleeves and told me that I would need to wear long sleeves in the future. I felt embarrassed and ashamed. It sounded as if she wanted to keep it a secret which made me feel like an outcast and I knew I had to keep it from the public. I was referred to a specialist. An appointment was made.

On the day of the appointment at a new clinic we arrived on time. I was very nervous. The surgery was on the first floor. I tentatively tackled the flight of steps, counting each step. It was a struggle but I managed reaching almost out of breath with weak legs. We walked into a beautiful and cosy reception area where a couple of people were waiting. The receptionist welcomed us with a warm smile. I reported my details and she asked me to take a seat. I had not been sitting for long when I heard, 'Miss Rickard, will you come this way'. I was taken down a corridor to have my lungs x-rayed, and blood tested after which I was taken to meet the specialist, a young beautiful, smartly dressed woman perhaps in her mid thirties. Her manner was as beautiful as her appearance. 'Hello, Karlene will you take a seat.' And she showed me to the chair next to her desk. I sat and we chatted. That helped calm my nerves. She later examined me and decided that I needed the lump removed urgently. The x-ray and blood tests showed that TB had missed my lungs which would have been lethal. Instead, it formed in a gland under my arm. However, I had to have it removed immediately. Around the same time the diagnosis from the gynaecologist was that I had one extremely large fibroid and several small ones which also needed to be removed immediately. Both clinics worked closely together and the specialists arranged for me to be admitted to Nuttal hospital where both operations could be done on the same day, one after the other. I would have preferred to be healed by a minister laying his hands on me and praying, but it was not to be. I consented to the operation, after consulting with Mom. She was both encouraging and supportive. The date and time were decided and I was admitted into the hospital.

Nuttal hospital is in a calm therapeutic setting and the staff and patients were friendly. On admission I was put on a short fast before the operation. Both operations were performed on the same day by different surgeons. They were successful. I was taken back to the room to recover from the anaesthetic. I was woken from a deep sleep by that familiar "voice" and my eyes focussed on the tube from the bag with the saline solution which was being fed into my arm. I noticed that the liquid was going below the safety level. I struggled forward and closed the tube. At that point I felt re-energised and I sat upright. The nurse came and was surprised to see me so alert. We spoke. Over the next few hours I got stronger and stronger. The stay in hospital lasted for three days. On the second day I was walking about, evangelising, about Jesus. Early the Sunday, which was my last day, I went to the chapel and I was there when Mom and Daddy Key came to collect me.

When I returned to Mom's I could no longer walk, my limbs were weak and I had poor bladder control. A young woman in her early twenties agreed to care for me. She was constantly at my bedside. She ensured that I was clean, tidy, fed and comfortable. When she was not busy doing things for me, she sat, held my hand and prayed with me. There was also a young man, who is now her husband, at hand to help wherever possible. On occasions they would take me for a drive to a mineral river. Dad gently guided me from the car into the river to a safe and comfortable spot where

I sat. The young lady took over and slapped my body with the water and exercised my legs. With time I got stronger.

One morning whilst Pastor Key and the brethren were praying, I had a desire to join them. I made my way by leaning against the wall along the passage that led to the entrance of a very large lounge/dining room. Everyone had gathered at the far end of the room. I was tired. I had already accomplished a lot. Pastor Key looked up and beckoned me. I made a tentative step but I felt I couldn't. The young lady was about to come to my rescue when Pastor Key insisted I had to do it alone. One step after the other I made it across the room. It seemed to have gone on for ever, but I made it. I could walk again. I spent six weeks, including Christmas, at home with the Key's and my son. Children and teachers from the school sent me gifts and letters.

In December I visited the specialists, who were pleased with my progress. I was prescribed a course of T.B. tablets for nine months, which meant that my stay in Jamaica was extended in order for the treatment to be completed. In January 1993 I returned to Morant Bay where I had been living since being on the teacher's exchange and resumed my teaching role in the village school where staff, children and parents welcomed me back and gave me a lot of support. I became more involved in the activities in and out of the village, attending Bible studies, music classes and visiting families in the village. On alternate week-ends I visited my son.

I spent the last few weekends of the exchange period attending a Bible course in the Morant Bay Town and doing the final rounds to say goodbye. On the penultimate week-end I decided to go to the village church on the Sunday to say goodbye. I Woke up early that morning and got ready. I could not find my Bible when I was about to leave, then I remembered that I had left it in the church in Morant Bay, the previous day, after bible study. I needed it. As the church was only five minutes away I had enough time to retrieve it. Furthermore it would be easier to get a taxi from that Morant Bay to the village.

On my way, about two hundred yards from the church, I was startled by a great bang on the corrugated fence to the back of a house next to the path. It was a little boy, about five years. He had jumped on the fence. I turned to look, as the tiny face peeped over the corrugated zinc and tiny fingers held on for dear life to the wooden panel that was visible through the gap between the zinc fencing. 'Miz, pray fe me' came his wee voice.

I wondered if that was the reason why I had to go to collect my Bible. 'I will pray for you.' I heard him drop from the fence with a thud.

Chapter 23

Standing alone

When I got to the church to retrieve the Bible, Sunday school had started. I was now torn between staying there for the Sunday school, which was always edifying, or going to church in the village. I decided to stay and enjoyed myself so much that I was making my way to the main service when I heard that "voice" 'Go to the village church in John's Town' so I slipped out of the building, down the side of the bank into the main road. Immediately a taxi came along.

'Are you going to John's Town?' I asked expecting him to say no as it was always difficult to get a taxi for the village. The road was in an appalling condition. During the week I had to charter a taxi and I had forgotten to make a similar arrangement for that Sunday. 'Get in' He said.

The ride was quick, but bumpy. I came out of the taxi at the side of the church, but walked around to the front door as the service was in progress. I slipped in discretely and sat at the back. Then suddenly I found myself arguing with the "voice".

'You will be a missionary, and you will be going on a missionary journey.' I thought about the brethren in my church, how well versed they were in the things of God.

I muttered, 'I cannot go on a missionary journey, I am not bright enough. I don't know the scriptures well enough.' Then I remembered what happened at my first convention in Minehead, Wales when God had called me to be a missionary and I reconciled myself to my fate and settled to listen. No sooner had I settled to listen to the sermon than I was invited to the rostrum to share from the scripture and to give a word of encouragement to the church. God enabled me to publicly declare His truth to those present.

The following Sunday I went to Mom's church in Spanish Town. She was preaching. In the middle of her sermon, she stopped, walked from the rostrum and stood before the pulpit. 'Sister Karlene, will you come so that I can pray for you. The Lord has called you to be a missionary to different churches around the world.' Obediently, like a lamb with a fluttering heart I walked toward her and bowed my head. Then, she said, 'Evangelist Francis (who was the secretary) will you write this down in the minutes.' She placed her hand on my bowed head and prayed. She then walked back to the rostrum and continued her message as if that period had not occurred. For the rest of the day I pondered over the experience in Minehead, then the church in John's Town's church only a week ago. I wondered what was next.

I did not have to wait very long. Before the week ended there was an invitation from Pastor Joseph of Nassau in the Bahamas. He had visited Mom's church some months ago and was a guest at her home. I was surprised that he had sent me a letter of invitation as I was not one of the ministers of Mom's church and we had not made any connection. Nevertheless I was grateful and excited. After all it had been a challenging year working in Jamaica and having had the operations I needed to get away to somewhere exotic before returning to England. I couldn't have imagined a better place to spend some quality time with Pianki. He had passed the common entrance exam. He was the only pupil from the church, of all those who had entered, to pass. Pianki's achievement resulted in him being awarded a place in Glenmuir High - one of Jamaica's distinguished high schools. My imagination came alive. Receiving the invitation, booking the flight and leaving for Nassau seemed to have happened very quickly. Before I knew it we had landed in Nassau.

The flight was very comfortable and I enjoyed the privilege of the wheelchair service. Pianki and I were chirpy. We laughed and joked with the porter as he pushed me along the corridor to the immigration section with Pianki holding on to the handle of the chair. We were about to go through a narrow passage when two male officers, one stockily built about six foot and the other shorter and quite thin, approached us. The taller man had an aggressive snarl on his face. He stretched out his right hand and said 'Papers'. They were given to him; he flicked through and came to a full stop on the letter, which he scrutinised carefully seemingly counting every word. He said something to his colleague and passed him the documents. He too looked at the letter carefully. I sat calmly looking at them, but out of the corner of my eyes I could see a uniformed lady looking across at us. One minute she was there behind the barrier, and then she disappeared. Almost immediately, she returned with another woman. Both walked boldly over to where we were and the uniformed lady took the wheelchair and spoke to the officer. Immediately my papers were returned and our journey continued through the barrier, then through a number of doors until we were in the arrival lounge. At that point the ladies exchanged smiles and the second lady, who was the pastor's wife, took over as the uniformed lady went back into the building.

I was taken to the car. Whilst inside the car I was told that the female officer came out and asked for the person who came to meet the 'woman of God' with a little boy from Jamaica. Apparently as she stood and watched the male officers about to harass me this stirred the Spirit of God within her and she heard an inner voice which said, 'I have sent my servant, get the lady who has been sent to meet her and collect her from the officers.'

Once settled in the car we started to praise God and continued to praise Him throughout the journey which seemed quite short. I was taken to a family - a mother and daughter in their small flat above a shop. The first night was tiring. Having just landed after a long day, I needed to rest, but the family was experiencing emotional upheaval and wanted a listening ear, and I was that ear. For the rest of the trip I was kept busy dealing with some of their personal issues.

On my first Sunday I went to church with them. It was a small quaint building perhaps three miles away. My hostess was the evangelist of the church. The membership appeared to be small. This was the smaller of their two churches. I had not seen the pastor as he was supposed to be ministering off the island. As we arrived at the church, my hostess guided me to a seat. My eyes followed her to the main door and I was shocked when the pastor appeared. He walked over to me, smiled and shook my hands saying, 'I am so pleased that you could visit us.'

He walked back towards the evangelist, and spoke to her. I could see that she was becoming annoyed. They walked into the little office at the side of a reasonably-sized rostrum which was designed like a boxing ring but came back out quickly. She walked briskly to the back of the church and sat down, her body language and facial expression displayed anger. I looked toward him. He beckoned to me and when I joined him at the door of the office I certainly was unprepared for the next move. He said, 'I have to minister in our main church this morning and I am asking you to minister here.' My legs wobbled. I wanted to say,

'But I don't know how to' but before the words could come out, he ushered me to the rostrum. There I sat alone, feeling tense and isolated. The last thing I wanted was to cause my hostess any discomfort. She sat quietly at the back whilst the Pastor spoke to the members and left.

The service began with prayer followed by some lively choruses. In the mean time I was crying unto God, to take control of the situation and to minister through me. I missed most of the singing as I was having a deep conversation with Him. Suddenly I became aware that I was being called to minister the Word. I stood up and walked to the pulpit. I moved with confidence, my legs were incredibly strong. I looked down at the small "pond" of waiting faces which I greeted. They responded with warmth, then I started the message and the words flowed freely and easily punctuated by the people's responses with 'Amens' and 'Thank you Lord.' With each moment my voice rose and there was a surge of energy passing through my body that I held tightly to the pulpit, like a boxer ready to attack his opponent. The message was short and poignant. It left me physically and mentally drained while the congregation was rejoicing. Because of my exhaustion I was moving carefully to my seat to avoid tripping over, when the pastor appeared again. He both looked and expressed his disappointment when closing the service because he had missed my message.

My time in the Bahamas went quickly. Pianki certainly enjoyed himself. On our last visit to the church everyone attended to bid us farewell and expressed their love and gratitude and made a special offering collection. It was a generous collection. I knew in my spirit that it belonged to the church in Jamaica. I exchanged the Bahamian money for American dollars and took the collection to Pastor Key.

It was not long after the missionary trip that I had to return to England, September 1993. I had had a wonderful year on the teachers exchange programme in Jamaica but I was going to miss my son and Jamaica. The experience was therapeutic. God was still with me and continued to speak in different ways.

I was back in the damp and cold of England and my legs were unstable, often throwing me to the ground or causing me to stagger like a drunken man. I prayed for early retirement so that I could spend more time in the Caribbean where I would enjoy better health and could at the same time, be with my son. My prayer was answered. My doctor and consultant were concerned about the regular falls and discussed the possibility of early retirement. I spoke with the union representative, made an application, provided the necessary evidence and was given early retirement. I was excited and decided to visit the island frequently and eventually take my son back to England to be schooled.

One Sunday morning I thought about my new found freedom. I had enough money to meet my needs, support my son and bless our church in Jamaica. I asked myself why I would want to stay in a cold and damp England, so decided that I would live in Jamaica. I was pleased with myself until I went to church. I was one of the Sunday school teachers and so after the morning service, which was a blessing, I stayed behind to teach Sunday school. The classes were held in the afternoon for two hours between services. The ministers went home after morning service and returned for the evening service. This particular afternoon I was about to teach my class. We sat on the rostrum. I heard when someone entered through the side door. I looked. It was Pastor T. She came into the church and walked to the back and stood at the bannister. She looked as if she were mesmerized. It caused me some concern. I excused myself from the class and went to the back. 'Hello Rev T, can I help you?' She turned and looked directly at me. Her stare penetrated my skull as if transfixed or in a trance for a few seconds. Then she came to, not really answering my questions. She said, 'Funny I had a dream last night and you were in it, but it does not even make sense, you are not to change your plan.' She then moved her head briskly from right to left then back to the centre causing her long hair to sweep her shoulder. After this she chuckled, looked at me became more relaxed, smiled and left me standing. As she went through the other side door, I stood for a while, feeling deflated. I understood the message, but I didn't want to accept it. I wanted to live in Jamaica, not just to make visits or to have my son back in England. It was clear I was not supposed to move to Jamaica on a permanent basis but I ignored that message. I later paid a very heavy price for my decision. But God has been gracious to deliver me, yet again.

Chapter 24

God delivers again

After regular visits, interacting with the brethren in the church and being extremely active in their missionary and educational programmes, I decided I wanted to spend more time with Pastor Key and the brethren rather than being in the United Kingdom. I shared my desire with Pastor Key which she in turn shared with the church. They were excited and prayed regularly for such a time. Unexpectedly the move came earlier than I thought possible. In a flash most of my belongings were being shipped to Jamaica. It all happened so suddenly that I had no time to think.

One day whilst in my flat in London preparing for a visit from a very close friend, Grace, whom I had not seen for a long time I had a telephone call from Pastor Key. She had arranged for a young man to collect my belongings, which were to be shipped, with his, the following week. No sooner had she spoken to me than he made contact. We spoke. I needed barrels to pack my things and he assured me that barrels would be with me within twenty-four hours and that there was no need for me to worry because my belongings would be in safe hands. Grace's visit became secondary. The young man was true to his words. He arrived with the barrels; everything was moving at the speed of lightening. I didn't bother to ask God for guidance. It seemed perfect. 'After all it was Pastor Key, a woman of God. God must be working out his purpose for my life through her, never mind what Rev T had dreamt,' was my thought. When Grace arrived I was knee-deep in newspapers packing and she helped. In the mean time posing the question which I didn't want to hear, 'Are you doing the right thing?' I ignored her. 'After all what does she know, not being a Christian' was my thought. I then started to spiritualise her visit, 'God had sent her to assist me with the packing.' The visit passed very quickly, we didn't spend any quality time together. I was about to leave my friends and family and yet I could not be bothered to say proper goodbyes. I practically dissociated from everyone. I was totally guided by Mom, even though that familiar and trusted "voice" had spoken to me; 'Don't relocate, move freely between the two countries.'

At times I questioned my understanding of that familiar respected "voice". I must have heard wrong. I could not see the point in me being in England, no longer employed, with a small pension which could keep me in Jamaica. Moreover, the weather and diet would be much better for my health. Just the opportunity I had longed for. Added to this, the brethren in the United Kingdom and Jamaica had prayed for me to go and live in Jamaica because they knew my desire and that I enjoyed better health there. My visit to the island since 1988 had been regular. Each time I returned my legs were much stronger.' Physically, mentally and spiritually I was much healthier, well loved and respected by the church and others in the community. I felt very special, I guess like a member of the royal family, a prominent figure, privileged to be coordinating many projects whenever I was there. Each time I visited my position was waiting and the reception was phenomenal. Mom would dedicate a reasonable amount of time in the service for the brethren to greet me, make presentations of various kinds and afford me the opportunity to express my gratitude.

At last, I had landed on the island. The church welcomed me home. They had a special celebration service. I really felt at home. My belongings had not arrived as smoothly as promised. I even lost some expensive items. But that was no major concern. I was home. Home at last. Within days I was totally involved in the social and educational development of the lives of the young people both in the church and the community. My core responsibility was to supervise a small day care programme with four children under three years old. I had two young ladies, members of the church to assist me. At first I was disappointed, I expected some prestige, to work with Mom as an assistant counsellor. Anyway I took the responsibility seriously, starting by introducing an educational programme for both the children and their parents. I believed that the children's balanced development should start from an early age and their parents should be actively involved. My concept was to develop a cross-phase programme between the nursery and preschool, catering for children from three months to six years.

I couldn't have started a better project. I was invited to a meeting about the programme for early childhood; there I discovered the government had appointed a coordinator to integrate nursery and infant education across the island. I was also completing the final module of my Masters degree in Education management. I had done the theory and now needed to apply it to a real situation. It was ideal. I was challenged, it was exciting. My imagination exploded. I could visualise an education centre governed by Christian ethics and principles to shape young minds.

I repented of my initial attitude and thanked God for his divine gift. Mom gave me the liberty to develop the programme as long as she was informed. That was not a problem, I lived in her home and I needed a sounding board. I constantly bombarded her with thoughts and ideas. Sometimes she got irritated with me. So did the young ladies. They had expected to feed and clean the children, but I made a lot of demands - having regular meetings, discussing ideas and eliciting their thoughts. I had many sleepless nights thinking through ideas. I was burning up with zeal. My thoughts and imagination kept running ahead of me. I learned to slow down to keep pace with the staff. They needed to catch the vision and take ownership of the project. At times it was frustrating, but I had to be patient. In time I could see their apathy changing into interest. We started to work as a team. Their confidence grew and the standard of the care and service improved. Other parents brought their children and Mom invested more money in upgrading the venue to the national standard.

I got the parents involved. I wanted them to take more responsibility in the emotional, mental and spiritual well being of their children from an early age. I introduced new and novel methods to keep them interested. It was still very vivid in my mind how many people, especially in England, had supported Pianki over the years as I struggled with the physical paralysis which affected my mental, emotional and spiritual states. I was grateful and wanted to give back, to share the love of God which had taken over my heart.

The children and their parents were taken on family outings; the children visited the National radio station and were interviewed. The icing on the cake for that day was when the children were asked to sing. We went into the studio. The tiny children were practically lost under the table. The presenter was beside herself with excitement, she kept saying, 'They are so tiny and beautiful'. As the children sang her eyes were filled with tears. The children were heard across the island of Jamaica singing to the nation. It was sensational. Both the parents and children were very excited. This boosted their confidence.

The radio-station trip was particularly memorable because our "Down Syndrome" student was mistaken for the leader as he was taller and older than the other children and he did not disappoint us. He responded appropriately to the producer with a hand shake as he extended his hand and he confidently answered all the questions. My heart was overwhelmed with joy. All the hard work had paid off. I had worked closely with the lad both directly and indirectly. The experience of being paralysed in my legs enabled me to understand the difficulties he had in coordinating his muscles, managing his body and all the frustration that came with it especially when trying to get others to understand him.

Eventually the staff took ownership of the project. Their attitude and behaviour became positive and we worked as a team without the constant warring. A beautiful fragrance of love and hospitality developed which made us extremely popular in the community. Our reputation drew new parents from outside. Since then the school has grown in number and status and is now a feeder school to an excellent Primary school in Spanish Town, Jamaica. Most of the original staff are still working there and they have acquired additional qualifications. In 2005 I was informed that the first set of students had done exceptionally well in their high school entry exams and one attained one of the highest marks on the island.

As well as the cross-phased education unit, I had to coordinate the summer project across four of Jamaica's fourteen parishes where our church had planted churches, plus devise fundraising activities for the missionary department. These were just a few of the programmes I set up and was involved in. Unfortunately, I got too busy to spend quality time with God. The praise, respect and love from the children and their families became my opium. My adrenaline was constantly at a high, I was too excited to sleep properly. In the middle of the night I jotted down ideas, even at the expense of giving special time to my son. Although my grand aunt lived some twenty miles away I could not find the time to visit or even phone her. I neglected all of my family for my "new" family; Pastor Key had become my idol and heroine. Each day my confidence grew and I bloomed like a precious rose and just wanted to do more. I became blinded and deafened to the voice and Word of God and lived for the popularity and the freedom to explore and experience the people. I certainly felt that I had arrived home for good. I was in my comfort zone.

The project was going well, lives were being changed, better relationships blossomed between parents and their children, the church and the families. I saw the joy on the faces of elderly grandmothers and grandfathers as they visited the education unit and spoke with the children. Despite my involvement and the successes there were times when I felt estranged as if I were not really a part, just passing through. It was scary. I guess even at that time although I couldn't understand what was going on, God was preparing me to let go of the project for the next task – the parenting programme. He was reminding me that everything we do is for a time and season. To accomplish the ultimate of our purpose, there are different stages; each experience makes us stronger and ready for the next phase until the final task is accomplished. I had become extremely comfortable and pleased with the success of the project so I fought against the warning not to become too attached. Mentally I was planning years in advance. I could see the development of the school up to ten years ahead, there was an effervescence of joy.

Suddenly the tide of success turned against me. The situation became toxic and there was a current of negative and venomous emotions from those around. I was afraid. In fact, I was terrified. My biological systems were affected. I was constantly rushing to the bathroom, with a weak bladder and being tearful and nervous. Desperately I sought approval from everyone like a young child crying for attention but I was ignored. Often I would sit alone with my hands on my head as tears washed my face. 'Where, where is my audience, where, where is my popularity' I bemoaned. I felt as if I were being bounced from one side of a wall to another, which made me dizzy and weak both in spirit and mind. There was a perpetual whirlpool of distress inside of my head. I kept screaming for help, but no one heard. I wanted to die. There was no longer any point to living. Everyday I lamented, 'How could I be treated in this way, surely I am dreaming. After all I am the golden girl, the blue eyed girl.' Once again I called to God. This time He seemed far away which made me angry and I stopped holding fast to the promises and principles in the Word of God. Yet I kept repeating this portion of scripture:

"For to me, to live is Christ, and to die is gain", Philippians 1:21

I wanted to justify my desire to depart from the land of the living. Eventually I had to accept that things had changed or rather I was being brought back to the path that God had purposed for my life. It was time to truly submit to God and be obedient, there was no choice. I remembered the calling at Minehead to be a missionary to churches around the world which was confirmed a year later when Pastor Key prophesied in the middle of her preaching that I must work with many churches.

Once I reached that point, hope was restored. God came to my rescue, but I had to go through the consequences of my actions. I experienced many trials, inquisitions, and condemnation. Sometimes I thought I was in a court of law. Often, I submitted to the accusations for things I had not done, in the hope that I would be forgiven and former relationships would be restored. There was a lot of anger. It was confusing. Love seemed to have changed to hatred. To be honest I could not fully understand how the love of God that I had found in His people could become so cold and callous. There was definitely a landslide in the relationships camp. Nothing made sense in the natural. I sank into the mire of rejection. Although I knew God was going through the experiences with me my anger still turned inwardly. I questioned my short sightedness, 'How could I have displaced my relationship with God to rely on others?' For a while the situation got progressively worse, I got bitter and resentful. I wanted to escape from the ignominy, shame and pain. My health rapidly deteriorated. Firstly my legs, then my memory. This made me very nervous. Hours were spent alone, often in floods of tears. I had lost a lot of weight – I guess an inexpensive way to slim! The days merged into each other. I had no reason to mark any day special.

Chapter 25

Not every goodbye is gone

On this particular Sunday in March, mothering Sunday in Jamaica, I dragged myself from the mire of self-pity with Pianki and went to the local church. It made me think of my mother in England and wish that I could be there with her. After the service mothers were invited to stay for a special mothering Sunday lunch. The tables were well laid out in the back of the church. We were ushered into position by the men. The atmosphere was pleasant, everyone was sociable and it was a very hot day. The meal was delicious. I tried hard to engage, but struggled. It got to a point when I felt weary with a heaviness of heart. I kept reflecting on all the mothering Sundays that I had spent in the Key's church and wanted to cry. They had been fun. I left the table, where the other mothers were enjoying themselves.

Pianki was standing, talking with his friends at the church gate. As I passed them he nodded and assured me he would be home shortly. I walked slowly negotiating the rough stony path. At last I arrived home. It was hot and humid. I made my way to the side of the house and reached into my handbag for the keys to undo the grills to the veranda. They were not there. I must have given them to Pianki. I wanted to go back and get them, but I was too tired; the journey had sapped my energy. I just had to wait until he got home, after all he promised to be home soon.

I stood in the blazing heat. It penetrated my body, from my head to my feet. At first it felt good, but the minutes turned into an hour and the heat became unbearable, making me restless. I got progressively angrier, tormented by the heat I loved so much. I kept shifting my position, one-minute standing, then sitting on the concrete manhole then standing again.

Up and down like a yoyo. The wait seemed like eternity. I suddenly felt depressed and wanted to end my life. I stood up and looked into the sky, as if looking into the face of God, 'Please take my life' I pleaded with a weak strain in my voice. I felt giddy, my legs folded and I collapsed into a pile on the gravel; everywhere went dark, my eyes were closed. I don't know how much time passed before Pianki got home but I have a vague recollection of him dragging my weighty body through the house. The distance from outside to my bedroom was a long way. I must have stayed in a state of semi-consciousness throughout the night. When I came to, it was daylight and I was surrounded by Rod the young man who sometimes stayed with us, Mrs B an acquaintance who was visiting from England and Pastor Key. Mrs B supported me sitting up whilst Pastor Key gave me a wash. She kept saying, 'It is okay now, your mother is here, I am going to clean you.' Once I was clean she dressed me in fresh, clean clothes. The experience brought back the memory of being kicked almost to death by my husband, which resulted in admission to hospital and being surrounded by a team of medical experts.

My thoughts were interrupted by the rolling of a heavy vehicle which came to a grinding halt at the gate followed by the slamming of the doors and footsteps moving through the house. Two figures entered the room, Pianki and the Guidance Counsellor from his school. He looked relieved, and the Guidance Counsellor smiled at me. Well this is what Pianki had to say about the whole experience:

It was a Sunday afternoon in spring 1997. My mother and I went to the local church and when the service finished I congregated with my friends in the church yard. When my mother came out of the church she insisted that we should go home together. I told her that I would catch up with her in a couple of minutes. Forty-five minutes passed quickly and I realised that I had the keys to the house and unless she had picked up the spare keys my mother would be unable to get in.

In those days we did not have mobile phones to contact each other at the drop of a hat, so I ran to Lewis Street where we lived. Those next five minutes felt like an eternity as I was wondering what fate my mother would have in store for me, for not only being late but also having the key and leaving her to wait outside. I climbed reluctantly over the barbed wire fence in order to stop the squeaky gate from "giving me away" and the barbed wire caught my groin but I was completely in stealth mode.

I took a crouched position as I glanced through my mother's bedroom window only to find that she wasn't there, so I then peered through my bedroom window, again she was nowhere to be seen. I skulked around to the back of the house but the bathroom was also empty. Just as I was about to enter the back veranda through the grill in front of the door, I saw my mother sprawled outside, on the gravel, in front of my very eyes. My initial reaction was that she had merely passed out due to her anger which might have caused blood vessels to burst. I shook her but she did not respond. I even tried to poke and tickle her but she remained still. As a last resort I swore out loudly fully expecting her to jump up and throttle me, or slap me, but to my disappointment there was still no response.

I stepped over her fragile body and opened the grill that protected the door to the veranda. I then tilted my mother on her side and tried to lift her. All I can remember was that she was so heavy I managed to half lift her on my back as her feet dragged along the floor. I carried her through the kitchen, then the living room and into her bedroom, where I laid her upon her bed as sweat poured down my cheeks. I sat on her bed to figure out my next move but my mind went blank. I came to the conclusion to change her into her night clothes thinking that this was the right and only thing to do, as we had no phone and the nearest person I knew was not at home on a Sunday afternoon.

After changing her I sat by her side gently shaking her for at least half an hour. When nothing happened, in my own naivety I went to watch Television, only to find that my mother had disconnected the plug in advance to stop me from watching it. I improvised by using a paper clip to link the plug to the socket, but as I plugged it in, there was a spark and the paper clip flew out burning a hole in my tracksuit pants and narrowly missing my skin. On days like these you feel nothing is going right, and no matter how hard you try there will be a repercussion for every action.

I then heard a noise from my mother's bedroom and ran quickly, to see what it was, sliding on the tiling and nearly colliding with the door frame on the way. Unfortunately my mother had not woken and it was merely a cow passing by her bedroom window scurrying in the bushes. I reached over and felt for her pulse on her wrist as I had seen on television programmes many times before. I was certain that I had felt something through her skin, only years later did I realise that it was her wrist bone not her pulse. Anyway I then took myself off to the kitchen to get some water. When I returned I tilted her weary head and dripped some water into her mouth. There was a groan which gave me a huge feeling of relief. I then decided to leave her to rest for a while checking on her every hour. The time passed very slowly. When the sun had set I knew it was ten pm and my bed time, so I grabbed my pillow and crashed out on the *floor next to my mother's bed so I could keep a check on her throughout the night.*

When I came to, the cock was crowing, and it was morning already. My mother looked peaceful so I decided to get up and get ready for school. I grabbed my lunch money from my mother's pocket and set off for school. I took my usual route walking the two miles as I did every day, the early morning sun was beating down on my head, and all I could think of was about my mother. I did not even bother to have an early morning swim at the canal as I normally did every morning, as I felt a heavy burden weighing down on my shoulders.

When I approached school the bell rang loudly so I hurried to class. As I sat I turned to a girl, perched on the wooden desk behind me, her name was Melissa. I gave her a scenario that in reality emulated my current situation. I asked her what she would do, she told me she would have gone to someone for help. No sooner had she said this, I packed my things and ushered myself out of the classroom straight into the guidance counsellor's office. I explained what had happened and she grabbed me and we both headed urgently back to my house in her car.

As we entered the house we saw Rod, who stayed with us, who had just arrived back, as we headed frantically into my mom's room we found two people tending to my mother. My guidance counsellor sat beside my mother and began talking gently to her. My mother's eyes flickered. Suddenly the mist which seemed to be hanging above me began to clear.

Once I was presentable, Ron and Mrs B supported me to the transportation. My limp legs dragged behind my body through the house down the steps and along the foot path. They felt like a sack of potatoes. Once securely placed into the jeep the rest of the passengers piled in for the very short journey to the doctor's surgery. I was attended to immediately, even though there were many people in the waiting room. I guess I was an urgent case. He examined my weak body thoroughly.

'You are dehydrated and your blood sugar is low,' he said as he wrote out a prescription and handed it to Pastor Key. 'Get this medication immediately.' he stressed. That was not difficult as the pharmacist was around the corner and it was not busy. The medicine was quickly dispensed and we left.

At home I was given the medicine and light soup with plenty of liquid. After a couple of days, I was able to get around the house unsupported but I was still a bit fragile, disorientated and dazed. I would often sit and stare into space.

Chapter 26

Not every shut eye ain't dead

One morning I woke up feeling as if God had placed His mighty hands around me. There was an inner feeling of 'love and peace'. Quickly I shouted, 'Thank you God for saving me from a difficult situation'. Saved again!! My hope in him was restored, but I still felt trapped, alone and afraid; so afraid. I wanted to escape from the house, the environment, the country. 'How could I get out of this predicament?' I muttered.

The beautiful house and the comfortable furniture meant nothing. The memory of my first stage of paralysis came stumbling back. There were all the material acquisitions, yet I felt empty. At that point I would have been happier in one room surrounded by peace and love. I recollected this verse of scripture, "What does it profit a man to gain the whole world and lose his soul?"

I cried out, 'Help me God, what can I do?' Once again He intervened. Each day I got stronger until one day I found myself as it were, washed up on the shores in the United Kingdom. It was incredible, I was given another chance. I was delighted.

It was amazing how it all happened. I was sitting alone on the sofa in the living room when unexpectedly, my cousin, phoned to inform me of some cheap tickets to England. I took the number of the agency and phoned immediately. The tickets were booked using my credit cards and delivered later that day. That was a miracle, as things are usually quite slow in Jamaica. I waited patiently for the time when I would leave. The weather, food and people which I once treasured, faded into the crevices of my mind. I wanted to be back in England, a country I had desperately wanted to put behind me from the day I landed in 1967. Poor health had deterred me from being as active as before. Yet, I was now willing to return. Anyway, I was confident that God would place me where I needed to be and would keep me through all adversities.

In England I found myself on the edge of a rock pool of my original church. I felt I had a little note impressed in the palm of my hand saying, 'Go in, this is where you belong.' I was once very active there and the brethren cared for me, but I was too embarrassed to return. The obvious thing was to make a clean break and to find a new fellowship. But I couldn't. I wrestled with the thought, but in vain. God had placed me there in 1988 in the safe hands of the late overseer G. He was no longer there, but I had to be. Our meeting after experiencing the 1988 hurricane Gilbert remained vivid in my mind.

The thought of returning was plagued with fear, shame and embarrassment. Yet, I felt I had to; it was a thorn in the flesh which I had to bear. Even before I left Jamaica a member of Mom's church, not knowing anything about my circumstances approached me and said, 'You must return to your church in England'. At the time I was taken aback by her statement. 'Why is this woman saying this to me', I whispered with annoyance. In my spirit I knew the answer, God was using her as a messenger, but that was not what I wanted to hear. I wanted a new life. Then I remembered an earlier experience whilst I was on the teachers' exchange programme in Jamaica. I found myself attending two churches which were separated by a main road. They had some major doctrinal differences and were in contempt of each other. At first I was not aware of the difference. I had asked Ma Lou in whose home I was staying to recommend a Pentecostal church when I was not able to be at Mom's church. She sent me to the Pentecostal Church in the town.

The first Sunday I attended, everyone was warm and welcoming. I enjoyed their Sunday school, the teacher was very good. The lesson was well paced, informative, and uplifting. After the Sunday school we had quite a long break before the main service. Most of us stood outside just talking in the beautiful sunshine with a cool sea breeze. The church was on a hill and on the other side of the road below, slightly obscured by some trees, was another church. They were singing. I was attracted by the hymns. I stood and listened until it was time for our service.

At the end of the service I left sharply and at the gate I encountered a woman who was coming from the other church. 'Hello', I said. She nodded and smiled. 'What is the difference between the churches?' I asked. She sped up. I had to push myself to catch her up. When she had reached a safe distance from the church she slowed down and fell in line with my struggling steps.

'What were you baptised in?' she asked.
'In the name of the Father, Son and Holy Ghost' I said.
'Oh, you are in the wrong church, you should be with us.'
'Oh', I said a little confused and wondering what the difference was. At the time I thought we were all baptised declaring the same belief. I later learned that they were baptised declaring the name of Jesus Christ only.

Anyway, based on what the woman had said I visited her church the following Sunday. The Sunday school was not as organised as the other church, the contents had not the same depth and the teachers were not as zealous, but the service was wonderful so I decided to do Sunday school in the Pentecostal church (Jesus only in Jamaica) and the main service in the Church of God.

Whenever I attended the Pentecostal church on Sundays, the brethren watched as I descended from the church, crossed the road and climbed the hill to the "Church of God" after Sunday school. Some weeks later the elders of the Pentecostal church started to question my baptism and beseeched me to do the "right" thing which was to be rebaptised into their doctrine. One lady said to me, 'Now you know the truth, why don't you baptise in His name'. Wherever I met members from the church they kept persuading me. No one from the "Church of God" questioned my belief. They were always happy to see me. I continued to attend both churches until I finished my exchange teaching placement. The experience made me strong in God. The most amazing thing happened. I found myself loving everyone instead of being afraid.

Various members from the Pentecostal church got impatient with me and expressed anger and unpleasantness but I displayed love and understanding. Some just ignored me in public. In remembering that experience I drew strength and decided to return to my church in England but I must admit I was still looking for a way of escape.

Going back to Worldwide Mission was not the only challenge. Pianki and I were homeless. Our short term tenants refused to vacate the property. They claimed not to have had ample notice. I sought legal advice and the legal system supported the tenants. It was a harrowing nine months of homelessness, not even being able to collect our post, news coming from the agency that the rent was not being paid, misuse of the property and overcrowding, five people in a small space. It meant I had to be paying for repairs. The boiler had broken and the walls were damp and covered with fungi. Being out of our flat, made enrolling Pianki for school quite difficult. A new and an unexpected chapter of my life had started.

Homeless. I was pursuing legal action for eviction of the tenant at a cost, whilst the tenant received legal aid in their claim against me! To add insult to injury the tenant denied us access to the premises so we could not collect our personal belongings stored in the cellar or even letters from the front door passage. Ankhara came to our rescue. She invited us to stay in her home. There were alternatives, the homeless unit, a flat on a difficult estate or with other friends. Ankhara's home was near to all the services we needed. It was spacious and comfortable. We had our own bedrooms and a common space. Ankhara not only opened her home, but made herself available whenever possible.

One evening she returned from work tired and hungry. It was evident by the way she tumbled through the front door with a weary expression. I was unwell. Pianki had booked a taxi. We were waiting to be taken to the hospital. The wait was long. Ankhara insisted that she would take me so that Pianki could go to bed. (His mornings started very early because he had to travel a long way to school, which required changing three buses). We set out immediately. When we got to casualty it was crowded. The wait was interminable – more than five hours.

Chapter 27

New beginning

Despite all the challenges God had provided Marcia, another friend, with an application form for the school Pianki attended. It was a well sought after school, unknown to us at the time. I had tried a couple of schools but they were full. Pianki and I completed the application form and returned it. About two days later he was invited for an interview but the date clashed with my appointment to see the neurologist. I spoke to Marcia about the situation and straight away she offered to accompany him.

Pianki attended the interview, it went well, but they wanted his exam results which we were still waiting for from Jamaica. They gave us a few days to get them. We tried, but had problems getting connected therefore the new school took over and made direct contact with the school. They were given a verbal report, and promised that the certificate would be forwarded. Pianki started the school on time and was able to do most of the subjects of his choice. The journey from Ankhara's home was demanding; he had to leave the house extremely early and he got home quite late in the evenings. Despite the distance and travel, we were grateful that he was given a place in such a prestigious school.

We lived at Ankhara's home for just over two months. The journey to church was arduous and tiresome. Public transportation was slow and sporadic. I was unable to attend all the activities and only managed the morning service. Every day I cried to God for help. I was becoming spiritually emaciated, and desperately in need of more spiritual food. My cry was for a new church, still being in need of a genuine excuse to exit the church. It was more a feeling of embarrassment than anything else. The ministers and brethren were visibly pleased to see me. But I told myself I was a misfit and no one noticed me. Some times I allowed myself to be confused; even developed a feeling of rejection. I often read erroneously into people's expressions. Gradually I isolated myself.

The case for the flat seemed never ending. The three month projected time was almost up and it was likely to take another three months if not longer. I wanted to relieve Ankhara of having us. I felt burdensome to her so I arranged an alternative accommodation; her one-bedroom flat in Walthamstow. Ironically it was the same dwelling in which I had refused to place my hand on her chest when the "voice" spoke. The flat was better located for Pianki and me. He didn't have to leave for school so early in the mornings and only needed one bus instead of two, or three. The tube station was within walking distance and was manageable for me. The trains to church were quicker and since returning late in the evening was safer, I started to attend some of the evening services. I knew God was in the arrangement.

The Bible states:

"Commit thy works unto the Lord, and thy thoughts shall be established." Proverbs 16: 3.

I committed everything to Him. Very soon one of the deacons who at the time lived in the same direction occasionally took me home. Despite all of this I occasionally wrestled with being in the church, telling myself I didn't really belong because the church had grown in many ways and I had abandoned the fellowship for another place. There was a "Church of God" fellowship literally two minutes walks away from the flat, which I had visited on several occasions, and had even attended their Alpha Bible course which was rich and powerful. The brethren and pastors were warm and friendly. Their services were vibrant and orderly with healthy teaching from the Bible. They offered a range of social and spiritual activities, but I couldn't neglect my church in West Norwood. There was no way I could leave, so I resigned myself to the fact that God had placed me there and his purpose through me was being fulfilled. Once I stopped struggling I became spiritually, physically, emotionally and mentally wiser and stronger. My confidence grew and my relationship with Christ became more intimate. There was a constant dialogue and my ear was more attuned. My journey so far started to make sense for which I rejoiced. I praised him for all the people he had brought in my life; even those who had caused me much pain. The revelation led me to look closely at prominent Bible characters who had lost their way because they were influenced by people around them. Some examples were Samson, David and Moses. This made me thank God more because I was given an opportunity to be totally submitted to Him.

In the midst of my praise, blessings came. I became eligible to apply to Motability for their three-yearly lease scheme for a new car. I was excited, having never been in possession of a brand new car before. There was however a problem coordinating my right leg as it was weak which meant I could neither manage a manual nor an automatic car. Anyway, I was not anxious because I believed that God had placed me in this position so all that was required of me was obedience. I applied to the scheme. Within a short period, of time, I was invited for an assessment at the Motability centre. The appointment was very early in the morning and the centre was a long way from home, but near to church.

It was incredible how things worked out. There was a taxi driver in the church whose wedding I had been involved in planning in Jamaica. He was happy to have me staying overnight with them and to take me to the centre early that morning. How good is my God! He left me at the centre where I sat and waited patiently. I was very nervous, not knowing what to expect. Eventually I was called. The day was spent going through a battery of physical, mental and psychological tests. It was a relief to finish, knowing that I had passed all of them, but the weakness in my right leg meant that I was recommended to have a car adapted with hand controls. At the time I hadn't given any thought to what it meant to drive using hand controls. A shock awaited me when I attended the first lesson that had been booked with the British School of Motoring (BSM). It was a disaster. The car swerved all over the road just missing the pavement. I was discouraged and wanted to give up, but the instructor was wonderful. He was caring and supportive, 'don't feel bad about your effort, everyone finds the first session difficult' he said, adding as an after thought, 'this car has a left foot accelerator, would you like to try it?'

To be perfectly honest I had no idea what he was talking about, but I said 'Yes'. He leant over to where I sat in the driver's seat and pulled down a left foot accelerator and the right pedal disappeared. 'Now try again using your left leg to accelerate instead of your hand. It was amazing! I took to it naturally. That was my answer. He smiled and so did I. 'Will you stop now please?' I was just rearing to go. 'We cannot progress with this lesson', he said. My heart sank. But before I could think the worse, he went on, 'I can see this is for you but you need to get in touch with Motability and inform them of the situation and then you will have to be re-assessed.'

'Assessed again,' I echoed.

'Yes,' He said. 'This is a different system.'

I really didn't want to go through the test again and the journey. 'Let me try again with the hand control', I insisted, but he would not hear of it. He was determined that I should reapply. I ambled out of the car and went into my flat with his words trailing behind me, 'just phone up and they will arrange everything'. I went inside and slumped on the settee. I wasn't going to bother. Suddenly I felt as if I were nudged in the side which made me jump to attention. I found myself saying, 'Okay Lord I will go and do it now'. I phoned the assessment centre and explained the situation. The person responded, 'We will be in touch'. The wait was long. I had given up looking for a letter.

One night I attended the local church. They had a visiting speaker. She spoke clearly and confidently with passion as one who was truly hearing from the Lord. 'I have a word for someone,' immediately my heart began to throb and I was convinced that God was about to talk to me. I listened keenly. The word was fifteen days of continuous fasting with fruit juice. There was no doubt, God had spoken to me. The following day I phoned Pastor G from my church and related what had happened to me. He did not question the validity of the message or the action I was about to embark on. Instead he gave me relevant scriptures and instructions on how to proceed and then prayed with me. The fast began. The first day was easy but the third I wanted to give up; I felt physically and mentally weak. Amazingly, on the fourth day I felt rejuvenated. I was no longer hungry for physical food, but had a craving for the Word of God and the need to be alone with him. I fulfilled both longings. On the sixth day I had a letter from the Motability office, requesting me to attend the assessment centre for reassessment. The date given coincided with the twelfth day of the fast. Already I was physically weak, and was getting weaker. Being shut in with God was okay, but how could I get to the centre in that state. The sensible and logical action was to ask for another appointment, but I found myself accepting the date.

On the morning of the appointment, I got dressed and made my way to the tube station, I felt strong. I had received supernatural strength. I got on the train and, throughout the journey I was in conversation with God. From the station I took a taxi to the centre arriving with enough time to relax. They kept offering me food and drink, which I can't remember happening so frequently on the first occasion. Anyway I resisted. The atmosphere was impregnated with percolating coffee, fresh cream cakes and *my bedroom window, again she was nowhere to be seen. I skulked around to the back of the house but the bathroom was also empty. Just as I was about to enter the back veranda through the grill in front of the door, I saw my mother sprawled outside, on the gravel, in front of my very eyes. My initial reaction was that she had merely passed out due to her anger which might have caused blood vessels to burst. I shook her but she did not respond. I even tried to poke and tickle her but she remained still. As a last resort I swore out loudly fully expecting her to jump up and throttle me, or slap me, but to my disappointment there was still no response.*

I stepped over her fragile body and opened the grill that protected the door to the veranda. I then tilted my mother on her side and tried to lift her. All I can remember was that she was so heavy I managed to half lift her on my back as her feet dragged along the floor. I carried her through the kitchen, then the living room and into her bedroom, where I laid her upon her bed as sweat poured down my cheeks. I sat on her bed to figure out my next move but my mind went blank. I came to the conclusion to change her into her night clothes thinking that this was the right and only thing to do, as we had no phone and the nearest person I knew was not at home on a Sunday afternoon.

After changing her I sat by her side gently shaking her for at least half an hour. When nothing happened, in my own naivety I went to watch Television, only to find that my mother had disconnected the plug in advance to stop me from watching it. I improvised by using a paper clip to link the plug to the socket, but as I plugged it in, there was a spark and the paper clip flew out burning a hole in my tracksuit pants and narrowly missing my skin. On days like these you feel nothing is going right, and no matter how hard you try there will be a repercussion for every action.

I then heard a noise from my mother's bedroom and ran quickly, to see what it was, sliding on the tiling and nearly colliding with the door frame on the way. Unfortunately my mother had not woken and it was merely a cow passing by her bedroom window scurrying in the bushes. I reached over and felt for her pulse on her wrist as I had seen on television programmes many times before. I was certain that I had felt something through her skin, only years later did I realise that it was her wrist bone not her pulse. Anyway I then took myself off to the kitchen to get some water. When I returned I tilted her weary head and dripped some water into her mouth. There was a groan which gave me a huge feeling of relief. I then decided to leave her to rest for a while checking on her every hour. The time passed very slowly. When the sun had set I knew it was ten pm and my bed time, so I grabbed my pillow and crashed out on the into the final stop.

'Whoh', I uttered when I saw the sign, I was miles away from home, had taken the wrong train and now found myself at London Bridge. By then I was really weak, tired and frustrated. With the last burst of energy I cried out, 'God, please give me the strength to continue.' From then on I became oblivious to my action. I have no memory of the journey from London Bridge to Walthamstow, but I got back home safely and sank into the enfolding arms of the armchair.

The success of the test meant that I could resume my driving lessons with the BSM, this time to learn how to drive using the left pedal accelerator when I phoned to book the lessons, the instructor on duty was the said one with whom I started and he was available to teach me without delay. I was indeed grateful. He had been an encourager and even though we had only met once I felt comfortable with him. We arranged the allocated number of lessons. I was excited and couldn't wait to start.

On the first day we greeted each other like old friends. I got off to an excellent start going from strength to strength. Each lesson went quickly. Before they were completed he got me to start the process of applying for my very own newly adapted car. That was useful as he helped me to make the right decision. I finished the driving course and collected my own beautiful new Starlet red car the following week. I sat inside and gave thanks to God. It smelt fresh. It was really beautiful. It was adapted to meet my needs. I now had no excuse not to attend my church in West Norwood some fifteen miles away.

It was so much easier driving to church. It was warm and comfortable and I did not have to leave home quite so early in the mornings. I could also attend activities at different times. This helped me to be more settled and I became a Sunday school teacher and a counsellor for new converts. Those individuals who had made a decision to accept and follow the teaching of Jesus Christ.

Counselling in the church opened a new world. I became more engaged with the word of God and with others in the church. There were opportunities to do "altar work" at public meetings in association other churches. On one occasion the meetings were run by Barry Smith (a well-known and established teacher of the Word of God now deceased) and Helen Shapiro. We were expected to serve at their altar, guiding and praying with new converts. The experiences were spiritually enriching.

I can recall a gathering in City Temple, a large church in Holborn, London. The counsellors met and prayed in a small back room. We were in unison. There was an awesome atmosphere. The auditorium was filled with singing and worship. We sat at the back as people filed in and took up their positions. Soon the pews were full and the service began. The atmosphere was absolutely electrifying. I took my seat at the back with the counsellors. I got lost in the praise with my hands lifted up and tears in my eyes. After the praise and worship the teaching began. There was much to take in. The teaching was on the "End Time". The speaker gave evidence, lots of details and facts. He taught with clarity, passion and sincerity. The Bible was his main tool; he was uncompromising about the truth. As he talked about the devil and the wickedness of current practices in society there was enough said to agitate and aggravate the natural man, to cause people to leave their seats and go to the altar.

I listened carefully. I reached the stage where I got lost in God. He enfolded me in His arms and I was safe. The speaker had scarcely finished and started to make an altar call when a current of people transcending age and culture flowed to the altar. As counsellors we joined them. Standing next to individuals, we were recognisable by our badges. We made ourselves available; once they were ready we found a quiet spot, took their details and gave them some literature. At the altar, shock waves just kept moving through me and I was covered with goose pimples. My heart throbbed with anticipation. I felt so privileged to be working with young people yet again.

Whilst living in the rented accommodation I was visited by five parents with their children. They wanted me to tutor their primary aged children in Mathematics and English. It was an unusual request given that three of the parents knew that I was a qualified secondary school science teacher and education manager. There was no other response but to say that I was not qualified for the job. Anyway, we discussed different ways in which they could be supported and eventually they left looking disappointed. Somehow I felt guilty, as if I should have offered more. After the last person went through the door, I went back into the living room and flopped onto the settee. I was agitated, afraid even. Was I disobeying again? was my concern. I slid from the seat unto my knees, leaning against the settee and prayed. There was that "voice" again, 'Start a supplementary school, King Jesus Academy.'

Later that evening I phoned Robert, one of the parents and a good friend who later became the cofounder of K.J. Academy. 'I thought about your request today, what do you think about us starting a family centre supplementary school. How would the parents' respond?' I could feel a warm smile on his face. 'I will speak to them and get back to you'. Soon a meeting was arranged at Robert and Yvonne's home and the concept was discussed. The parents needed no persuasion. They were keen. K.J. Academy was born. We were all excited.

The date and time of the launch was decided. It had to be held in Robert and Yvonne's home, but there was only one qualified teacher, me. At that stage they were recommending qualified primary school teachers which I thought was ironical since they could have approached those teachers in the first place to tutor their children. It was then I became absolutely convinced that God wanted me to work with those particular parents and Robert in establishing a supplementary school.

I took the teacher's details and promised to make contact. Unfortunately, they were too busy at the time to become involved. Once again I called on God for a teacher. He brought Rita, a secondary teacher with a wide range of teaching and counselling experience to mind. We had not been in touch for a while, but I knew she was not in full time employment and was currently doing private tuition. I believed God wanted Rita to be involved. In the meantime, I asked Clare an excellent Primary school teacher to help with the initial planning, to update me with what was happening at the primary school stage. Although she was busy, she made time for us to meet, discuss and plan.

Eventually I made contact with Rita and told her of our intention. She sounded interested but wanted to meet for further discussion. We agreed a date and time. That evening I sat on the settee waiting for her. The time came and went. I got on my knees and talked with God, 'You promised Rita, yet she has not kept the appointment or even phoned.' Then I sat down again and focussed on something else. Minutes later the door bell rang. There stood Rita before me looking a little tired. Before greeting me she blurted out, 'Would you believe it, I made two attempts to get here but I got lost, so I decided to go home. I went into the bus station and my bus arrived but I could not get on. I tried but I was being prevented. It was really strange. I had to come back. I walked out of the station and felt as if I was led by the hand straight to the door. Here I am.' I smiled at her, 'Come in Rita.' She came in and sat down where I had been sitting. I shared my experience. She just laughed and said I will help with the Saturday school. I can't remember what else we spoke about.

The school was launched and we worked with the whole family-parents, teachers and students, a big happy family. The work was exciting. It kept me sane because it distracted me from the legal process in regaining my flat. We worked hard to develop KJ Academy.

Whilst living at Ankhara's she brought me an application form to apply for a grant to run a project of my choice. At the time, given my situation of being homeless I hardly wanted to think of engaging in any project. I just wanted to move into my home. She kept pressing; she became a pest and at times I wished I was not living there. To avoid any negative repercussions, I gave the form some attention. Then I remembered saying confidently to the brethren in Jamaica, during a difficult meeting in which I was being judged unfairly, 'I am going back to England to be the best in parenting.' I don't know why I said that and what it actually meant, but somehow I was convinced that I was going to make a significant difference to thousands of families. After I said this I had peace of mind.

On reflection I thought 'Parenting' was the project, but to be honest I really wasn't keen on starting anything - too much was going on for me. Ankhara asked me if I thought about a project. She was tenacious. I told her about the parenting project. Perhaps it was my way of saying thank you to all those who had supported Pianki whilst I was ill. She thought it was a brilliant idea and her mind started to race ahead. It was tiring just listening to all she had to say. Once she finished, I put down the form and relaxed. Ankhara never gave up, she kept nagging, nagging, nagging. So I took up the form again and it was then I noticed that they had given three different dates over a period of one year for the completed form to be submitted. 'I have plenty of time' was my appropriate excuse for delay.

Eventually I moved to her one bed-roomed flat, still waiting for my situation to be resolved. But Ankhara never gave up on the project. Whenever she visited, which was quite often, she asked about the form. One day, in an angry tone she said,' I won't ask you about that project again'. I could sense that she was hurt and very disappointed in me. When she left that evening I felt guilty so I went in search of the form. The place was in disarray, I couldn't imagine finding the form, but I found it easily. I had missed the first two dates and there were two days remaining for the final submission. As I held the form I could hear Ankhara nagging. For peace sake, and because I did not want to disappoint her, I read through the form and completed it. After all she seemed to have faith in me. The form was badly hand-written, untidy with mistakes. I was too ashamed to ask her to check it. I knew she would be angry. It was unsatisfactory but I posted it anyway. Within a short time I had a reply accepting the proposed project.

It was then I became interested and was motivated to move forward. I shared my good news with Ankhara and asked her to be my mentor, which was one of the requirements to the millennium award project. She was elated. As a matter of fact, so was I. We were given dates to attend various preparation meetings for the project. At the meetings we received training and had to make presentations. Ankhara was very impressive. Many of the project leaders wished they had her help and some envied me in having her as mentor.

Following the meetings and training we met regularly and discussed the project, planning a series of workshops on parenting issues, our focus was on identity, emotional influence in effective parenting and community support given to families. We worked well together, it made us even closer.

The project was advertised nationally and launched in January 2000 in Waltham Forest. I felt so proud. People from different places in the UK responded to the advert and wanted me to set up the project in their area. On the day of the launch the turnout was good. It was well organised and looked and felt extremely professional. The key speaker had the participants sharing their cultural journey. It was powerful, everyone was engaged. It was an emotional time for all and the evaluation was encouraging. Everyone wanted extra sessions and for them to be longer, and they committed themselves to attend the remaining three sessions.

The project was scheduled to take place over six months. From the feedback it was clear that I needed to develop a lengthier parenting programme. The parents welcomed the concept of a 'Modern Village' where they would be able to support each other and acquire additional parenting and relationship skills. The thought of the amount of work that would be needed caused my spirit to wane. I didn't feel ready to take on that commitment, still being a little fragile and recovering from some of the negative experiences I had on my journey back to working with the community. Anyway, my thought was that when God places one to do a job he ensures that all the essential doors are opened 'on time'. He is an "on time" God.

I arrived at their office very early on the Tuesday morning. It was next to the training rooms. The office was closed. As I waited, the trainer Dr Marilyn Steele arrived. Our time together was invaluable, we bonded. Eventually the office staff arrived. They were eager to meet me, especially Pat with whom I had conversed. She was also on the course, in fact so were most of the staff. I thrust myself into the programme and became an active participant. I felt as if I were there from the beginning. Toward the end of the week I approached Pat and asked her if she would co-facilitate the programme with me; co-facilitation of a thirteen week - three-hour parenting programme was a part of the course. 'Thanks, but it would be impossible for me at this time, my baby is due in October and there are so many demands on my time.' I smiled.

Within a couple of weeks, I recruited enough parents to deliver the programme and to my amazement Pat requested to join me. We co-facilitated the first Strengthening Families Strengthening Communities Parenting programme to be delivered in the U.K. Six years later, in 2006 Pat and I were the first to deliver another family programme, My Mum and Dad Argue A Lot by "One plus One". The evaluations were excellent. One person called us a perfect double-act based on the way we delivered the programme, sensitively, professionally and effectively, keeping everyone feeling safe and enjoying ourselves while being respectful and supportive of each other.

One day I was sitting in that familiar spot on my bed when the phone rang. It was one of the chief wigs of the organisation who found and brought the writer and trainer of the Strengthening Families Strengthening Communities parenting programme to England to train facilitators. He said, 'I would like you to send us a profile of yourself and Robert, (cofounder of KJ Academy). Our organisation would like you to accompany me to Atlanta to deliver a workshop at an international fatherhood conference if our proposal is accepted.' I could hardly believe the words coming through the telephone receiver. I got excited and wanted to tell everyone. I contacted Robert immediately as he was on his way to Africa on a missionary programme. He accepted the offer, but I had to organise our profile. I set about putting the paper-work together and posted it to the organisation. I mused over the generosity of the air fare and all the expenses being paid for one week by the organisation. About three weeks later I was in the same spot when I had a call from one of the employees to confirm the trip and to inform me of various preparation meetings and arrangements.

I arrived at their office very early on the Tuesday morning. It was next to the training rooms. The office was closed. As I waited, the trainer Dr Marilyn Steele arrived. Our time together was invaluable, we bonded. Eventually the office staff arrived. They were eager to meet me, especially Pat with whom I had conversed. She was also on the course, in fact so were most of the staff. I thrust myself into the programme and became an active participant. I felt as if I were there from the beginning. Toward the end of the week I approached Pat and asked her if she would co-facilitate the programme with me; co-facilitation of a thirteen week - three-hour parenting programme was a part of the course. 'Thanks, but it would be impossible for me at this time, my baby is due in October and there are so many demands on my time.' I smiled.

Within a couple of weeks, I recruited enough parents to deliver the programme and to my amazement Pat requested to join me. We co-facilitated the first Strengthening Families Strengthening Communities Parenting programme to be delivered in the U.K. Six years later, in 2006 Pat and I were the first to deliver another family programme, My Mum and Dad Argue A Lot by "One plus One". The evaluations were excellent. One person called us a perfect double-act based on the way we delivered the programme, sensitively, professionally and effectively, keeping everyone feeling safe and enjoying ourselves while being respectful and supportive of each other.

One day I was sitting in that familiar spot on my bed when the phone rang. It was one of the chief wigs of the organisation who found and brought the writer and trainer of the Strengthening Families Strengthening Communities parenting programme to England to train facilitators. He said, 'I would like you to send us a profile of yourself and Robert, (cofounder of KJ Academy). Our organisation would like you to accompany me to Atlanta to deliver a workshop at an international fatherhood conference if our proposal is accepted.' I could hardly believe the words coming through the telephone receiver. I got excited and wanted to tell everyone. I contacted Robert immediately as he was on his way to Africa on a missionary programme. He accepted the offer, but I had to organise our profile. I set about putting the paper-work together and posted it to the organisation. I mused over the generosity of the air fare and all the expenses being paid for one week by the organisation. About three weeks later I was in the same spot when I had a call from one of the employees to confirm the trip and to inform me of various preparation meetings and arrangements.

The workshop was more like a seminar with over fifty delegates from different parts of the world attending. The evaluations were very good. One of the delegates, Janet, came from Jamaica. She showed a great interest in my work and we developed a positive relationship.

There were further advantages in doing the parenting project and the Saturday school, I became known and associated with the large established parenting organizations in the UK and Jamaica. National Family & Parenting Institute, a parenting organisation launched and established a parenting week programme in October 2000. They invited me to their reception in the House of Lords. At the time I was experiencing difficulties with walking and wondered how I would be able to attend. When I phoned and explained my situation without hesitation the director said, 'We will arrange for one of our cars to collect you.' As time progressed I was invited to the House of Commons on two occasions.

I presented various parenting programmes and participated in discussions with two Caribbean islands about the parenting programme being delivered on the respective islands. I am confident I will be working with them in the future.

Chapter 28

Ushered into purpose

After we successfully completed the course I went to Jamaica for my vacation. Whilst I was there I introduced the programme to the Early Childhood department. They had scheduled a series of workshops which included three on parenting. The trainer for the parenting sessions was experiencing some personal difficulties so I was invited to do the workshops. The sessions were well received. Some days later, I spent some time planning a parenting programme proposal with the coordinator for the island's early childhood trainer. It was a very productive meeting. She welcomed the delivery of my programme on the island. I was excited by the prospect of working on the island as has always been my desire, but God keeps sending me back to England.

I reflected on my journey. It seemed ironical given the chequered history in my own parenting experience, that I would become such a strong leading force in the parenting programme both in Jamaica and the United Kingdom. My ongoing illness meant that I had become dependent on many individuals to support me and Pianki.

Each day I had a better understanding of how God's purpose for my life was being accomplished. Every battle, hurdle and experience equipped me to work with families. My past was determining my future. The ability to love unconditionally, to give, be patient, tolerant, listen and validate and not be afraid of criticism were all part of my training. I couldn't believe the change in me when I considered how rigid and afraid of criticism I had been.

Whilst making preparations in the office for the delivery of the Strengthening Families, Strengthening Communities Programme, I met an old acquaintance, a member of the church. She recognized me immediately, but to be honest I didn't recognise her at first. We had met years before we both became Christians. We actually remembered our meeting on different occasions, which was strange. She connected me with a community organisation for which I worked and I remembered her on a more personal level and connected her with parenting. We met at a party. I was impressed by her wide knowledgeable, eloquence and sociability. At the time I wished I had a small portion of her skills and abilities. Some weeks after we had met, I needed a baby-sitter for an evening and she came to the rescue.

Since then we had lost touch. It was good to meet again. She shared much about her faith and her business and all she was doing. I was humbled by the fact that she thought I was skilled and eloquent enough to become a trainer and wanted to introduce me to different openings. Most importantly to know that she had become a vessel to be used by the Lord, I could hardly contain myself. Bubbles! Bubbles! Bubbles! but the lid of my emotion remained in place. We parted. I finished the programme and went to Jamaica.

Much time had elapsed. It was Mothering Sunday, 2001 when we met again. I was invited to dinner by a member of the church. Although I had planned to be in my church on that Sunday and the distance to the lady's house was very far, I still accepted. I left church straight after the service and drove steadily arriving at my venue within an hour but earlier than agreed. To my surprise my old acquaintance was there. When she saw me she emanated a radiant smile. We greeted each other like long lost friends and sat sharing experiences oblivious to our hostess and her mother who were preparing the meal. We were locked into our own world. On reflection I wondered what our hostess must have thought of us. We were invited to a well spread table of delicious food. There was lots of laughter and fun. The meal was absolutely wonderful. At the end of the evening, in true Caribbean style we received a 'goody bag'. To conclude a perfect evening my acquaintance prayed a special prayer for me. Before we parted she mentioned a trip to Ohio, she had booked an extra bed in her room and welcomed anyone who was willing to travel with her. I showed a genuine interest. I knew nothing of the place or the conference of which she spoke highly, but I felt a need to be there. I found myself saying, 'I would like to come but I am not financially able'. We parted.

Some days later she phoned and wanted to know whether I was serious about going on the trip. I reiterated my position, to which she retorted, 'I didn't ask you about money, the lord will make a way.'

'Yes I would like to go.'

'Okay I will finance the trip.'

I accepted. She gave me the dates of the conference and when I could travel with her to spend time together, before the conference. Meanwhile an anonymous person had sent me an application form from an independent consultancy in parenting for another large reputable parenting organisation. Apparently there were sixty places but more than five hundred applications were sent out and over one hundred were being interviewed. I was successful in my interview but the date of the induction programme and the conference clashed. I decided to travel anyway. The flight was booked. The package included an additional stop in Atlanta for over a week. Within a couple of days, the air tickets arrived in the post.

I arrived in Ohio on the Friday with the understanding that the conference would be on the Sunday. Doreen, the friend who invited me, phoned in the night and informed me that the conference began on the Saturday. I must admit to feeling a little disappointed because I had wanted to explore the area on the Saturday, however, I arranged for a taxi to get me to the church which was some five miles away.

The driver left me at the front entrance and drove off. I walked to the front door where a lady was selling programs. It was really quiet. She asked, 'You here for the conference?'

'Yes.'

'We don't start until tomorrow.' I turned to watch the taxi disappear along the main road. The place was isolated and I wondered how I would get back.

'How can I get a cab?' She asked the time and then said,

'If you don't mind waiting for an hour I will take you home.' I was happy to wait.

As we were talking, another lady arrived to register. She had booked to stay on site. We started talking. She had travelled from Arizona which just so happened to be where Pianki was about to attend the University for a semester, on an exchange programme with his university. She had lived in England for many years before moving to Arizona. I told her about my son and she was happy to be a contact for him. I was excited about the support for Pianki. It is always difficult to adjust to new situations so a friendly face makes it much better. The new acquaintance made the journey worthwhile.

After talking to the lady from Arizona I went for a stroll around the complex. I stumbled onto a restaurant where there was a hive of activity in preparation for the following day. I found a seat in the sun and got comfortable. Despite all the activities I was at peace. In fact, it was over two hours before I was collected but I hardly noticed the passage of time. My new friend, whose name I have forgotten, drove me straight to a restaurant as a treat for being patient. We had a wonderful meal then she dropped me home and arranged to collect me the following morning for the conference.

When I entered my hotel room, I was shocked to see that my belongings were missing. I phoned reception to make enquiries and was informed that Doreen had arrived and being dissatisfied with the accommodation had booked me into a different hotel. My things had been moved and Doreen had left instructions at the desk for a taxi to take me to the new hotel. As I had gone directly to my room I hadn't received the message. The time in Ohio was certainly filled with lots of excitement and blessings. Doreen and I had a special time. Unfortunately, I never saw my new found friend, who looked after me so well on the first day, again.

Soon after we returned to England, from the conference, I was called by God to go to Jamaica. The immutable God, the El Elyon, summoned me. I was terrified. Jamaica had become a hot furnace for me. I had disassociated myself from family and good friends and had dedicated my time and energy to the people in Pastor Key's church. They had become my new family, but for some unknown reason they had tossed me aside. It was hardly the place I wanted to return to. But the Lord had not tossed me away. He promised to provide for my every need.

Chapter 29

God has not given us fear

December 2001 I returned to Jamaica. Once again The Lord told me to book my flight. I was reluctant, but heeded to that familiar "voice". This time I had absolutely no expectation. I just surrendered to His mercy and direction, my faith was extremely high. I listened keenly to His every word, being careful not to be influenced by friends, family or the church. I watched God's mighty hand at work. As various needs arose in my life they were met.

On arrival on the island, I heard the voice of God. There was clear instruction not to go directly to May Pen, but to stay at Sis Malcolm's home in Kingston. I asked my Pastor friend to take me to see her. It was the first time I had ever visited Sis Malcolm directly from the airport. The amazing thing was that she had actually prepared for me and before I could say thank you for having me, she started to praise God and thank Him for allowing me to be in her home. Both she and her husband treated me as an honoured guest. She took me to church where I was asked to minister the following Sunday. It was not a surprise because God had birthed a topic in my spirit and I felt at peace. The following Saturday, the night before the service I locked myself away in the comfort of my room to prepare the message, on the topic that He had given me. Suddenly another topic came into my spirit. I became confused. I thought, 'it is not like God to change His mind', but I prepared both messages. By the break of day, there was a call from the pastor who collected us, 'Sis Karlene we would like you to minister tonight' - that was the reason for the second message!

Whilst in Kingston, there was no time to become bored or discouraged. I was asked to attend an official forum on parenting. As I shared my heart I felt the anointing of the Lord. I attended a church where I ministered to both parents and children on the parenting role. As a result, an organisation requested for me to attend their retreat as a trainer. During my stay in Jamaica I was given the words, 'In a little while ……….' God opened some incredible doors. I was asked to work on my parenting programme for Jamaica.

After leaving the island, and returning to England, I continued to develop my parenting programme. I saw how it could become an international programme impacting the lives of individuals irrespective of their race, culture or belief system. The prospect of empowering families drove me to work extremely hard in making the programme a reality. I engaged with different specialists and experts as God opened the doors. The feedback was extremely positive and enabled the programme to evolve.

Chapter 30

Value in counselling

The parenting experience made me realise how much counselling was needed both for me and those with whom I worked. In the past I had been a sceptic in regards to counselling, especially cross-cultural counselling. I had heard of too many black people been wrongly diagnosed and treated as mental cases. I regarded it as the first stage to hell. However, as a true scientist, I felt that as I was doing a research project on the role of counselling, I needed to understand more about counselling in order to make an accurate judgement. To do this I needed to pursue a counselling course. Therefore, I completed the foundation stages both in Christian and secular counselling. I saw the merit of this because after all counselling is a biblical practice. In Proverbs 11:14 it is stated, 'In the multitude of counselling there is safety'.

In delivering the parenting programme I realised that a solid background in counselling would be advantageous. It would also augment my personal journey. The illness had affected my mental state. Friends and family had focussed on my physical recovery but had neglected the importance of my mental state. In the church the brethren cared for me. They rejoiced and glorified God for the physical progress I made in being able to walk unsupported, moving up and down hills on the mission field. Alone I struggled with low self-esteem, lack of confidence and courage. There was a constant battle within. I was afraid to make my voice heard. Prior to my illness a lot of emphasis and expectation was placed on what I had achieved academically. The struggles I was actually experiencing were overlooked. If only they could have heard and felt my heart's cry, I thought. I just wanted to be allowed to get in touch with my feelings and cry and be open to someone without being judged or condemned or pitied. I needed unconditional love and empathy.

To satisfy those around me, I was forever performing and always ensured I kept 'me' safe. The blessing of being able to travel between the United Kingdom and Jamaica, made it much easier for me to manage the pressure of demands and expectations. In Jamaica the environment, weather, food and the presence of God were all wonderful, but the brethren just did not understand. When I wasn't busy working I isolated myself. This was often perceived as me not being myself. I needed someone to help with the emotional and spiritual journey.

I tried unsuccessfully to find a Christian counselling course. Daily I cried out to God to provide the best way forward. As usual he answered in His timing and the way He deemed appropriate. Unexpectedly whilst back in England, there was an opportunity to pursue a certificate in counselling. I went for an interview without having paid the prerequisite fee which at the time I could not afford. After the interview I was offered the opportunity to do the diploma once I had completed the first year. I explained my financial situation which included the non-payment of the initial fee. The head of department who interviewed me understood and wanted me to pursue the course. She advised me to speak to the learning support officer who could help me to access the financial assistance for students experiencing hardship.

It was a wet day. It rained continuously. As I entered the office, there was a torrent. The rain came harder and faster as if I were being sent a message. The wait to see various people was not frustrating. I was shut in which was a better alternative to wading through water. In the office the necessary forms were completed. When everything was done and I was ready to leave, the rain stopped. Some weeks later I received a letter offering full financial support for the course. I accepted the position, but instead of the day course which was my original intention I opted for the evening one. Every Wednesday evening for the year that I attended it rained. Even if the day was dry it rained in the evening. Rain is now an indicator of success for me.

The training was excellent. I learned a lot and I worked through a lot of my personal issues and was able to share Christ with others. One young lady accepted Christ as her personal saviour. We developed a friendship which was therapeutic to both of us. She was the primary carer for her mother who was permanently in a wheelchair. I was able to share my experience of being in a wheelchair and this helped her to understand and care for her mother much better. Their relationship improved. The year was a resounding success. My personal growth and development were exceptional; I developed a special love for people. The ending of the course coincided with me travel to the international Fatherhood Conference in Atlanta and other engagements. There was no closure at the end of the course which concerned me. Unfinished business had become a pattern for me and one I wished to dispense with.

Although the counselling course was a tremendous blessing, I was convinced that God had made it possible. There was a time when I thought I should really be in Bible School, studying the Word of God or doing Christian counselling so I did not commit to pursuing the diploma in the second year. Additionally, the places were few and the tutor made it clear that there was a waiting list.

Once again doors opened after I returned from Atlanta which had been a fantastic experience. I was called to attend an interview for the second year. There were a large number of applicants but I was offered a place. The costs, including travelling expenses and books were met by the college. I knew that it was God's hand.

The demands of the course were phenomenal. My faith was challenged, and I had to hold fast on to God's principles, admitting my limitations and not being afraid of my vulnerability. Often my views and beliefs placed me outside the group consensus, but I felt loved, respected and admired me for my integrity, gentleness and sincerity. In fact, that was what my fellow students said. The experience helped me to be grounded. I appreciated everything I learned. Subsequently my faith grew stronger. One aspect of the counselling course was to arrange placement in one or two recognized counselling organizations. The arrangement could include up to twenty percent of young adults between 17 - 18 years old and eighty percent adults. I decided to do eighty percent bereavement counselling in Whipps Cross Hospital and the twenty percent in an 11 - 16 girls' secondary school which was within walking distance from my home. Both places were, in fact, within walking distance.

I phoned the Head and arranged to meet on the Monday. I knew the school well as we'd had an educational working relationship for many years. I arrived on time for the appointment and was met by the Head. She was relatively new to the school, but I had worked with her in another school.

We went into her office where we had some pleasant exchanges before discussing the real purpose. Pat was warm and friendly. She welcomed my desire to work with them; she was convinced that I was the right person to help a number of the African-Caribbean girls who were struggling in different ways. I said to her I am allowed to do twenty percent of the hundred hours with young people between 17 - 18 years. 'Okay', she said, then you are required to do eighty percent with us.'

'No' I said, only twenty. She looked confused and I could not understand her difficulty in comprehending what I was saying. Then it dawned on me the upper age in the school was 16 so I could not do my placement there. I just smiled, explained the requirement of the course and extended my apology. Somehow I was disappointed because I felt God wanted me to work in the school. Pat was also disappointed as she wanted me in the school. The discussion shifted from the counselling to the parenting programme. We agreed to have a further discussion at a later date. Before leaving her she recommended schools in which she thought I could do my placement. She had a lot of respect and appreciation for the work I was doing and wanted her colleagues to benefit. The schools Pat suggested were familiar, but I was not interested. There was a conviction in my spirit that I had to work in Pat's school. I thanked her and left.

When I got home I sat at the familiar spot on the bed and mused over the blunder I had made. Whilst doing that the "voice" said, 'You must contact CSCT.' This was the counselling board and to be honest I was not sure what I was going to say to them, but I phoned. I had a rather odd response from the course manager. My question to her was, 'Would it be possible to work with young people sixteen years old for the twenty percent of the placement. She was a little abrupt and rude 'Have you not read the criteria for the course?' A fair question I guess. 'No, not as yet, I am still waiting for them' I said. Her tone became more conciliatory; she went on, 'As from this term the full 100% of your counselling can be with minors as long as you are supervised by a qualified supervisor, accountable to the Head of the school and who is familiar with the Children's Act.' It was too good to be true. After putting down the receiver I shouted a big 'thank you Lord.' To me it was evident that God had purposed and charted my path. Immediately I phoned Pat, who was pleased. We arranged another appointment.

I discussed the new criteria with my course tutor, who decided I could only do a maximum of forty hours in the school as the college was not comfortable with their students doing all minor counselling since the course was more designed for adult clients. I was contented with that. A week later I met with Pat. We discussed the relevant details and I established a counselling service in the school. I offered each prospective client ten sessions, each an hour long. It was incredible how effective the service was, in such a short time the lives of the girls were being turned around, one girl made a 180 degree change in a positive way.

The counselling course continued to aid my personal and professional development. It gave me permission to be myself, to be real and to face my life with honesty and truth. I could really say that a godly character was being perfected in me which was obvious by what the Bible identifies as the fruit of the spirit for example love, kindness, patience, meekness and so on.

During the class sharing and discussions I spoke about the miracles God had brought about in my life's journey which impacted the lives of my colleagues. Personal counselling over thirty hours was an integral part of the course. The journey with my counsellor was invaluable. She was able to guide me professionally at the same time enabling me to work through personal issues based on identity and relationship. After each session I felt I had a thorough emotional cleanse.

Chapter 31

Forever mysterious

In the early part of 2002, I was alone in my flat just reflecting on life as was often my practice, when that familiar "voice" spoke, 'You must to go to Barbados.' Just then the door bell rang, it was Ankhara. We had not seen each other for a while. It was good to catch up; so many things had happened. Among the flow of everything she said, 'I need to visit schools in Jamaica and Barbados to do some research as a part of my MA programme.' I could not believe my ears, I found myself saying 'Can I come?' That was rather strange as four weeks earlier I had turned down an offer to travel to Jamaica with Dee. I had used every excuse possible to convince her that travelling to Jamaica at that time was not safe. Eventually we agreed to postpone the trip until the following year. Yet there I was almost begging Ankhara to travel with her to both Jamaica and Barbados. It caused me to question my longing to spend time away with her. Whilst analysing my reaction, I was stunned when she said 'Yes, you can be covered by the grant.' I went absolutely quiet, almost holding my breath. I expected her to say, 'Sorry, I am just joking', but she was serious. We started to discuss the practicalities of the trip. She left me to arrange the flights and contacts with the schools in both Barbados and Jamaica. I could not wait for the next day to get started. The violence in Jamaica, which I had used as an excuse with Dee, was no longer a deterrent.

At the break of day I was ready. It was a very successful day. I managed to provisionally book our flight and arrange times to visit schools in both islands. I was eager to update Ankhara on the progress made, but try as I did; I could not reach her. She was like a needle in a haystack. I became extremely frustrated and as time progressed my frustration turned into anger. Time was passing, we were supposed to be leaving for the half term which was around the corner and I needed to confirm the flight and pay the deposit. Just as I was about to give up she phoned. By now my spirit had dampened but I tried to disguise my hurt as I shared the progress. Somehow she seemed uninterested. She had apologized for being out of circulation. From what she had said, it seemed that she was under pressure so I put down her lack of enthusiasm to tiredness and stress. The conversation ended without any decision being made, but she had promised to phone early the following week. She did. I was deafened by the words, 'Ofsted'. The school in which she was working had been scheduled for an Ofsted inspection after half term. Apparently the head said that the senior staff could not travel. I wanted to blurt out 'You are a liar. You just don't want to travel with me'. Instead I gripped the receiver tightly and lay back in my bed. I felt my heart stop for a moment. I did not want to believe what I was hearing. She paused as if wanting me to speak, but I remained silent, so she continued, 'We could go somewhere else for a short break,'

'Okay' I said, putting down the receiver and began my usual analysing. Why? Why? Why? I asked myself. Once I stopped feeling sorry for myself, there was a recurring thought in my mind, 'you must go to Barbados' I could not ignore it, so I audibly questioned myself, 'where will I go, with whom will I stay, why would I want to go by myself'. There was no answer, but within my spirit I felt I had to go. The truth was, I had no means of financing such a trip. Anyway, having learned from experience, by faith I reserved a flight. The following day Ankhara phoned and I told her what I had done. She sounded more excited than surprised. 'You can stay with my parents. I will phone my mummy and let her know'. It was amazing how quickly everything was finalized. I was going to spend time with Ankhara's parents whom I had not met and did not know. All I needed to do was to phone her mother with my flight details. I did. It was as if she were waiting eagerly to see an old friend. I confirmed and paid for the flight with my trusted friend 'Mr ACCESS, the credit card.' I still wasn't sure why I was going to Barbados alone to stay with an elderly couple for such a short time.

A few days before travelling I contacted the Multiple Sclerosis society for financial support to have the necessary adaptations to the new car through the Motability scheme. The officer said it wasn't possible to help with the car but if I was interested they would pay for a holiday to the sum of what it was costing to go to Barbados. Naturally I accepted. My flight was covered. Later that day I went to dine with Ankhara, a farewell meal. After we finished eating she passed me some money which I thought was for her parents, 'That is to cover your keep'. She said. I shoved it back. She looked surprised. The atmosphere changed and things got tense. I was uncomfortable and embarrassed, perhaps a little angry. I needed financial help but I didn't want her to feel that I was depending on her or that she needed to compensate for not travelling with me. As we sat quibbling over whether or not I should accept it, I remembered an experience I had two weeks previously. A young brother whom I take to church regularly made a contribution towards my petrol. I refused. He said to me, 'Why are you taking away God's blessing from me.' It is written in our manual, the Holy Bible that it is blessed to give. That insight made me accept his contribution and Ankhara's. She looked relieved, but I was still not all together comfortable; however, we enjoyed the rest of the evening together.

I arrived in Barbados. I felt a little disappointed. Looking through the window of the plane the terrain looked flat, arid and uninviting, unlike Jamaica. At that moment I wondered what the trip was all about. It was too late to do anything about it. The plane parked and we disembarked. I remember marvelling at how quickly I got through immigration, not like the protracted procedure in Jamaica. Collecting my bags was easy, the process cheered me up. I was impressed. Soon I was out in the heat of a calm and attractive airport. Ankhara's mom had no difficulty recognising me. She rushed over and hugged me tightly as she repeatedly said, 'Welcome, welcome, welcome'. The warmth from the sun, her embrace and the atmosphere certainly made me feel at home. We got into her cousin's car and made our way to the house. As we drove along the highway, the cool breeze bathed my face, it was refreshing. Her cousin was very friendly and we got involved in a deep conversation about God. Before I knew it we were home. I was shocked when I met Ankhara's dad, he looked like my own dad- same complexion and manner of dress. He was waiting for us; regrettably he couldn't come to the airport but was eager to meet me. We became very close. I felt like a daughter and a member of the family.

On the third day the most incredible thing occurred. It was around 10.00 am, I was alone with my new father. Ankhara's mom had left the house early to check their tenants. I was sitting on the sofa in the middle of their rather long through-lounge, facing the veranda. The morning was cool and I relaxed, enjoying the moment of tranquillity when I heard a muffled sound, I turned my head in the direction of the sound to see Ankhara's dad coming from the bathroom in a daze, clutching the waist of his trousers, staggering into the passage. Before I could finish saying, 'Dad are you okay?' he was lying flat on his back, eyes closed, body slanted, where he had fallen through the doorway from the passage into the lounge. His head just missed the low wall which separated the passage from the lounge. A few items came crashing down with him. His head and trunk were in the lounge and his feet in the passage. My heart missed several beats. 'God, it is you and me!' I shouted, stooping to cradle his head in my arms. I was frightened. 'Please be merciful to us God' I whispered with tears streaming down my face. Gently I replaced his head on the floor and stood up. For a moment I panicked, unfamiliar with the house and the country. I rushed into the bathroom where I got smelling salts for him but there was no response. Then I went and phoned a couple who once lived in England, but had returned to their native land. They were the only contact I had. The wife answered. I composed myself and explained the situation to her. She guided me. I acted on the guidance. It was such a relief when his eyes opened and he started to mutter a few words. He wanted to go to the bathroom. We struggled but somehow managed to go to the bathroom and then to the bedroom. I phoned the doctor, who was far from helpful. In the middle of the crisis two men came to change the gas cylinder and the dogs went berserk. Dad muttered, 'They won't get past the dogs to change the gas cylinder.' It was the last thing I wanted to hear. By now my legs were weak and I was getting tired. 'Please, God will you help me?' was my plea. I could hear the gas men; they were banging the gate impatiently. I managed to steady myself to walk to the veranda to arrange another appointment. As I got through the door one of the men put out his hand for the money. They had already changed the bottle and were waiting to be paid. That was the easy task! I just smiled thanked the Lord and went to get the money. They left and the dogs calmed down. It was at that point that it became clear why I had to visit Barbados; to be there for Ankhara's dad. About two hours later Mom returned. She entered the lounge looking tired but smiling. By now Dad had had something to drink, his blood sugar was reasonable, and he was resting in bed. I was back on the sofa totally exhausted. 'Dad collapsed and his blood sugar went below two' I said. Without another word she went straight into the kitchen and prepared his meal. It was ready in a flash. She took it into the room and fed him. Then she returned and gave me something to eat and we sat around the dinner table. It was at that point that I realised how scared she was. She had been in a state of shock. 'Thank you Karlene, I don't know what would have happened if you were not here and I came back to find him lying unconscious in the room'. We sat and stared at each other without a word. For the rest of the holiday I spent most of the time with each parent in turn. Dad would not go out without me. I had really special time with mom whilst she cooked and did chores around the house. On occasions we went out as a family shopping, to the beach and other events. I had a wonderful time with my new found family, but I learned not to be too attached; God had sent me there for a purpose. I have later discovered that Ankhara's dad no longer suffers with diabetes.

Chapter 32

Another mystery

Yet another trip, in the same year 2002! I had already booked my flight to Jamaica when Pastor G announced that he would be taking a party to Jordan and Israel, weeks before my trip to Jamaica. I have always wanted to visit Israel and Pastor had taken many parties there. Several times I started the process, but the trips always clashed with me going to Jamaica. I was always torn, saddened that I had to choose, but Jamaica always won, leaving me feeling guilty. This time I should have felt reprieved, as there was serious military and political unrest in the two countries and human beings were being decked with explosives and used as human bombs. The tourists' presence in Israel had decreased dramatically. It was reported on the National News that towns and villages were decimated daily leaving mounds of rubble; school buses packed with young children were being blown up.

The situation was critical, yet Pastor was going to travel with a party to both Jordan and Israel. It was his first trip to Jordan. On the face of it, it seemed unwise. Who in their right mind would travel with him? The announcement had hardly left his mouth when the "voice" spoke. 'You must go on the trip.' I tried hard to ignore the "voice", but I got progressively hot and my head felt as if I were on fire. Once again I said 'Yes, Lord'. Immediately I turned to Mother Popplewell, a mother and friend (we sit next to each other in church.)

'Mom I have to go on the trip.' As the words left my mouth my temperature returned to normal and I felt at peace. My next move was strange. My financial situation was not in a healthy state but I reached into my handbag for my cheque book with eagerness to pay for the trip in full.

Everything was odd, I don't travel around with my cheque book, but I had it that day.

I was excited about the trip and couldn't wait to tell friends and relatives. A trip to the Holy Land, to walk where Jesus walked, where He healed and talked with people. It would be awesome. I was having a living experience of being with Jesus in my mind. Everyone I told responded negatively and could not understand why I should want to visit Israel at such a time. Some of the comments were.
'Are you mad?'
'Do you know what you are saying?'
'This is not the appropriate time!' My prayer partner said. 'Karlene this time I have to pray for you because you are not thinking straight.'
I was not deterred by people's attitude and behaviour. I knew that God had spoken to me yet again, and when He spoke the plan would have been in place for His purpose to be accomplished in my life. So I kept my peace. Selah.

Cocooned in my own world of faith and belief, each day I got more excited, like a child whose parents planned to take him/ her to Disney land, wishing the days would pass by quickly. I packed well in advance of the day. Each day the News of the unrest got worse. The violence had intensified and tourists were not being allowed in the country. It was the major point of talk among the brethren. Many were sure Pastor would cancel the trip; he had gone to minister in South Africa and was due to return two weeks before our trip to Israel. This left me confused as I was absolutely positive that God told me to travel. I questioned myself; had I heard from God? Why has God impressed upon me to book for a trip that would not take place? Anyway, I consoled myself by saying 'God wanted to test my obedience.'

When pastor returned from South Africa he announced that despite the rumours the trip was still on and he would not be deterred from doing God's plan. On hearing the announcement, I felt as if my kidneys, intestines, bladder and other organs leapt for joy. I imagined what it must have felt like when Mary the mother of Jesus and Elizabeth the mother of John the Baptist were pregnant and met for the first time, and John jumped in his mother's womb. Once again my mind was at peace, but suddenly walking became more strenuous and I needed to go to the toilet frequently. Despite my strong faith, I was concerned about my mobility. I became even more weighed down when I attended our preparation meeting; the itinerary was intense and included lots of walking and excursions. I could not see myself being a member of the party. Just imagine a woman in her forties moving like a snail and needing the bathroom every second deciding to explore Jordan and Israel with a group of young fit vibrant people in a war zone where there were regular news flashes of human bombers exploding, killing others and themselves. To make it worse there were land mines and a heavy military presence. Despite that rather grim picture I was ready. I knew I would not be travelling in my own strength, but in the strength of the Lord.

At last, the day of departure arrived. Robert, my good friend, took me to the airport where I met the rest of the party. I had not requested the wheelchair service which was unusual, given my pervious experience. I felt supernatural strength surging through my body. Proudly I strutted down what seemed an endless path using my umbrella as a walking stick. At times I struggled a little and felt some pain in my legs, but I enjoyed the challenge. I guess I could use the aid of a walking stick, but I wanted to be like everyone. I had not eaten that morning; I was full with child-like excitement. By the time I got onto the aeroplane I was quite famished. The flight was not the most comfortable and the food not appetising, but the thought of being in the Holy Land appeased my disappointment.

We landed safely and went through immigration without any problem. Passing from the cool building into the warm night air I felt like an amphibian that had been energised, ready for action. We all piled into the comfortable coach and headed for the hotel. In the hotel lobby we were introduced to our roommates. My roommate Jo was a young woman about 5'ft 5'in. She looked strong with a well-built body. I had seen her nearly every Sunday in church, but we only greeted each other from a distance. She was a gift sent from God. On that first morning, before breakfast Jo offered to massage my legs. She took each in turn and massaged them as they have never been massaged before. After breakfast she got me some water and Jordanian currency, all that I needed for the trip. The first part of the excursion was on horseback, to the mouth of The Siq, a narrow 1.2 km (miles) gorge hemmed in by 100 m cliffs to the main entrance into the city of Petra. It used to be the stronghold of the Nabataeans, an early Arab people. Petra was renowned for its massive architecture and the ingenuity of its dams and water channels.

I had not ridden for a long time. Initially I was nervous as I could not feel the animal's body next to my legs. I gripped the reigns and begged the guide not to let the horse go too fast, when it started to canter along the path. The thought of that enormous animal galloping down the slope and being thrown to one side on the dry sharp rocks filled me with terror. But the guide was careful to keep the animal under control. It cantered on the uneven surface causing my body to bob and sway in the saddle. I grinned to myself. Then my confidence started to grow. 'Can you stop for a moment please and take a picture of me?' He kindly brought the animal to a halt and took the picture. For the rest of the journey the guide stopped periodically pointing out historical sites and rare species of plants. It was fascinating. When we reached the entrance to The Siq, I dismounted, a little disappointed. I had hoped to make the whole journey on the horse. At this point my roommate was ahead, I needed her supportive arm to walk along The Siq. Before I had time to concern myself about her absence, God provided a lady my age with similar interests. We shared experiences as she became my companion and walking stick. She was strong and healthy. Timely we made the journey, a little distance from the main party but near enough to hear what was being said. Each time Pastor stopped to point out the magnificent carvings in the naturally pink rock we were right there. I would sit for a while to recover before continuing the track. The path narrowed as the cliffs seemed to close behind us, then it widened in front. It was amazing. Patiently we followed the path. I drank every drop of the history that I could contain. There were even fig trees growing between the rocks. It was absolutely fantastic.

We must have walked through the cliffs for about two hours looking at the elaborate carved façade which depicted gods and mythological figures. Then we entered an opening which was breathtaking, it was an ancient temple, with a flight of steps cut into rock across a court yard. The area was bustling with activities, vendors with their wares and men with camels touting for business. I welcomed the bench, which was an addition to the historical site for tired tourists, giving the camel ride a miss to take a well earned rest. It was hot, causing me to perspire profusely and drink a lot of water. At no time was there any urgency for the bathroom, which was unusual. I sat and watched as the camels folded their long giant legs underneath their bodies making it possible for individuals to mount into the small saddles perched on their backs. Then they rose triumphantly, one after another towering over everyone. We all laughed as the animals were led across with their passengers. We spent sometime in the courtyard where we rested and purchased some souvenirs before moving on to another site with a restaurant and toilet facilities. It was the first time since we left that I felt the urge to use the bathroom. Although the queue soon lengthened

I was blessed to be allowed in early, after which time was spent eating and socialising. I made my way back through the cliffs with the same gusto. I really saw God at work in my life.

The next day we had an equally challenging journey. We ascended to the great height called Mount Nebo, possibly to the spot where Moses (who led the Jewish people out of Egypt through the red sea and into the wilderness) stood and viewed the Promised Land. Unfortunately, Moses was not allowed to enter in because He displeased God when the people tried his patience. He lost his cool and acted contrary to God's instruction. I stood and faced the Promised Land, peering into the distance. It was a vast plain. I felt a churning in my stomach. I smiled to myself. I was excited and grateful that I was privileged to be looking at the Promised Land and within a few hours I would be walking the terrain.

As I stared in the distance there was that "voice" again, 'Ask Pastor to pray for you.' Immediately I scanned my surroundings to locate Pastor. He was a short distance away talking to two ladies. Without hesitation I went over to him and said, 'Pastor could you pray for me, please.' Amazingly, he took me back to where I stood initially, placed his hand on my head and prayed. It was a prayer of thanksgiving. He thanked God for my life and that the promises for me were being fulfilled and that I would enter the Promised Land. He thanked God for giving me the gift of counselling and teaching of families and asked that they would be perfectly developed. When he finished he noticed that two ladies with whom he was speaking earlier had drawn closer to us. He invited them to come and pray with me. Again he reinforced aspects of the previous prayer for me and then asked God to fulfil His promise for their lives.

Pastor finished praying and the ladies walked away. My whole being felt light as if I could have flown across the gulf that separated me from the Promised Land. I stood and looked in the distance; the area was veiled by a blanket of mist. I could no longer differentiate the land, but there was inner peace and a mighty presence as if a warm comforting arm was thrown around me. I knew God was within me and His presence was there. I was ready to make the journey. Slowly, counting my steps I walked toward the building where many of the brethren were viewing historical relics. I went into the building. It was cooler than outside and buzzing with activities. Various people passed by me pointing out things of interest, but I had a mindset to be in the Promised Land where the next phase of my life would become clear.

God was taking me through an experience where I was learning to be totally dependent on him; to walk alone with Him. Since the trip started, I had some strange experiences. Two different ladies came alongside me and were very helpful. They met some of my physical needs, becoming my human walking stick while I, in turn ministered to them. I was pleased that I had met such nice people and was looking forward to a deeper relationship. But on both occasions the ladies started to distance themselves and I felt like a leper. I could not say what went wrong or how I may have offended. In fact, those two ladies became good friends with each other.

Yet another lady, one that I would not have expected to befriend me, drew near. She willingly extended her arm to give me support. She replaced the other ladies. I took hold of the arm of my companion. We chatted as we walked timely down the slope from Mount Nebo we viewed the landscape around and stopped under some of the magnificent trees that embroidered the path. My eyes went to the spot where the coach had parked next to a Jordanian restaurant on top of the platform of another mountain. Suddenly I was jolted by voices behind us. It was the voices and footsteps of my two original companions striding pass. They were laughing and enjoying being together. They barely noticed me. I felt on the outside of their circle, discarded and thrown to one side. Strangely, I wanted to scream. Thoughts of me always being alone flooded my mind. My relationships are so brief, there is no permanency, people come and they go. It pained me, if only I could find a quiet place to go and cry, just to release the tension. I gripped my new arm support tightly, looked into her eyes and smiled, she responded with a gentle smile and we continued down the slope.

Eventually we all gathered at the bottom of the slope in front of the restaurant. The view as far as the eyes could see was of mountains and valleys undulating into the distance. It felt as if we were in the middle of nowhere. Once our Pastor and our guide agreed the eating arrangements we all filed into the restaurant which looked like a long tent positioned on the edge of the plateau. Inside, it was spectacular, like a spring in the dessert. There were comfortable chairs around tables to seat small and large groups. The décor reflected the culture of the Jordanian people.

There were long banqueting tables with creatively arranged healthy fresh salads, herbs, baked breads and large pots with steaming stew, roasted legs of lamb and other meats. There was an abundance of food. The atmosphere was impregnated with a fusion of aromatic spices. In groups we took our seats, I was at a table with five others which included my 'new arm'. I hesitated to call her a friend as my relationships have been too transient. After the meal was blessed, we helped ourselves; the choices were phenomenal making it difficult to choose. Once we were fed, watered and emptied we set out on our last leg of the journey in Jordan, to the border with Israel.

From the conversation I overheard between our Pastor and our guide it was clear that time had lapsed and we would not reach the border before it was closed. For the first time I acknowledged that we were in a political and religious contentious period and we were at risk of being hurt. I knew that God wanted us to make the journey and for me to be a part of this group. But for a moment I was looking at reality. Quietly I prayed and asked God to ensure that we got over the border without any difficulties. As I breathed out the last word of prayer I felt at peace again and the "voice" assured me that it would be okay. I looked across to the Promised Land and was confident that I would enter it. We climbed into the coach as the engine revved. The driver positioned himself and we started to ascend, spiralling around the mountain. As we moved into the valley there were vast expanses of arid land. Our party was lively, chatting, praying, engaged in many activities. Where I sat I could hear some discussions about the border being closed, but our leaders were calm.

Hours passed. At last we arrived at the border. It was closed to the public but opened to diplomats. The atmosphere changed inside the coach, everyone sat still almost if we had stopped breathing. Our guide who was efficient, kind, warm and friendly went outside with our pastor and we all sat and waited. They returned with good news. Our travelling documents were upgraded to diplomatic status and we were now granted permission to cross the border. Our party breathed out a great big thanks to God. As we crossed the border the bridge was covered with a heavy military presence. We were stopped by soldiers with their rifles and had to alight from the coach. They checked every corner of the vehicle. Once they were satisfied, we were allowed to board the coach and complete the crossing. The distance across was short.

Once on the Israeli terrain the coach parked near the immigration building where we had to collect our luggage and go through immigration to be checked in. They examined our luggage, passport, asked personal questions and scrutinised us. The security was stringent. Finally, we were through to meet our new coach, driver and guide. The heat was intense; it felt as if every cell in my body were on fire. I remembered experiencing something similar as a young girl in Jamaica; it was so hot that the tarmac on the road melted and we had to avoid walking on the road in the midday heat. Somehow this heat felt hotter. I could shed my usual extra clothing. As the heat permeated my body I started to feel comfortable and at home. To me it was evident that my days of living in a cold country were numbered. For a moment I was in ecstasy, I started to dream of the days when I would be free of coats and heavy outer garments, but was soon brought back to reality when we were ushered into our air conditioned coach. The driver and guide greeted us, they seemed friendly. From there we were taken to our new accommodation. I was still sharing with my initial roommate; our relationship was not as we began. But, I remembered how on the first night together in Jordan she had massaged my legs and then we shared the word of God. I could not have expected more. It was absolutely fantastic. I felt like running the marathon, praising God. How I wished she would just grab my legs again and give them a good rub. It was not to be. The relationship was a little estranged. She was polite and supportive, but I could feel her heart was no longer with me. I was alone. We were together in one room, yet separate. In the dining room we sat at different tables, mixed with different people, went in and out alone. Despite the estranged relationship with my roommate I bore no negative feelings toward her. Increasingly I started to feel the strong presence of God in my life. I held onto the passage of scripture pertaining to Joseph where he was sold by his brother to strangers and he said it was meant for good.

Our first visit, in Israel, was to Jerusalem. We travelled for a while, always ascending as Jerusalem was quite high above our hotel. Although the coach was full, I felt alone but I knew that God was with me. As it ascended and spiralled the hills I took in the view of the sheep pastures, expanse of wheat fields, and dwellings which accommodated the people known as the Bedouins who were similar to those known as nomadic. Soon the loneliness faded into insignificance. I started to connect the view and knowledge being shared by the guide, and others in the coach, with passages I had read in the Old Testament (the first thirty-nine books of the Holy Bible). These passages came alive. To see the wonders and miracles of God was just awesome.

We arrived at a pinnacle, the highest point in Jerusalem. The coach parked. Everyone alighted. The view was spectacular. We could see all around us. It was like sitting at the tip of a tower. We could view the Old and New buildings in Jerusalem, the surrounding walls and the temple. The party was organised to descend a distant path along a wall to the garden of Gethsemane. I desperately wanted to make the journey and individuals were prepared to support me, but I decided to stay in the coach and drive around to meet them at the bottom. Naturally I had to wait for them to do the journey. I sat for a while in the coach, then went and stood at the gate of the garden when it was nearly time for them to arrive. As I watched the group joyously descending it left a bitter taste in my mouth. I was jealous. I could hear the "voice" saying you could have done it, not in your strength but in mine. I got quite annoyed with myself, 'If only I had', I whispered to myself. But it was too late.

Everyone gathered in the garden. They were radiant; there was a glow on their faces. I got more upset. I really regretted my decision. I knew for a moment I had allowed my faith to wane and I robbed myself of a glorious experience. From that moment I was determined that once again I would be obedient to the voice of God.

The next stop was The Western Wall. In the midst of the Old City in Jerusalem is the section of the Western supporting the wall of the Temple Mount which has remained intact since the destruction of the Second Jerusalem Temple (70 C.E.). It became the most sacred spot in Jewish religious and national consciousness and tradition by virtue of its proximity to the Western Wall of the Holy of Holies in the Temple. According to numerous sources, the Divine Presence never departed. It became known in European languages as the "Wailing Wall". The Western Wall Plaza, the large open area that faces the Western Wall, functions as an open-air synagogue that can accommodate tens of thousands of worshipers. Prayers take place there, day and night, and special services are held there as well. Men who would like to go to the wall must wear a hat or take a free head covering from a box beside the entrance to the prayer area. As we approached the plaza I could see women everywhere praying. Everyone had a head covering. When we were nearer I could see a dividing screen that separated the men from the women. It was a sight to see bowing heads and hear varying sounds. We spent some time just looking and soaking in the atmosphere, then went on to the tomb and the area called 'Skull' where Christ was crucified and buried.

The journey between sites on the coach was trouble-free. The few coaches around were being used to ferry children to and from school. Apparently many places including the tomb opened to accommodate us because of who our Pastor knew. The terrorist activities and recent spate of human bombers in the city of Jerusalem had deterred visitors and affected the tourist trade. It was not profitable for the sites to be opening as frequently as they were used to.

Everything seemed so private and personal. I felt blessed and extra special. In each place there were but a handful of visitors and the locals. We were warmly greeted and the proprietors were grateful to see us. I was convinced that God had prepared this trip especially for me. Had it been normal activities with the volume of bustling human traffic, I would not have been able to get about with such ease or to absorb so much. The experience is beyond verbal expression. I can only say I was moved both spiritually and emotionally. I stopped observing a lot of the physical features and went into a deep spiritual experience. I felt at one with my saviour. To be walking along the path and visiting areas where Jesus, my saviour, had been, seemed too good to be true. Each day I felt closer to God. I felt that I would be more than happy to live there for the rest of my life.

The trip to the Dead Sea was absolutely fantastic. Again the low volume of human traffic afforded me easy and quick access to all the facilities that were available. Not being a swimmer, I was at first a little scared about going into the Dead Sea, but there were individuals to help me in. As I immersed myself in the water and my body floated to the surface, I felt as if every damaged cell within me had been healed. After the initial struggle I went in and out of the silky dense salty water several times with no need to queue. Each time it felt as if the electrical charges heightened in my body and the healing power continued. I went and wallowed in the black mud, like a hog. Growing up in Jamaica I used to stand and watch the hogs covered in mud. I would just laugh. Here I was covered from head to toe, including my teeth. The mud caked to my body. I felt cool and I relaxed until it was time to wash it all away. I could have stayed longer but I wanted another dip in the Dead Sea and to finish in the Spa. When I washed away the mud I was sure that the old layer of my skin had been removed and I was totally regenerated. My final experience was relaxing in the warmth of the sulphur mineral Spa. At the end of all the activities my skin felt like velvet, my joints were painless and my body was totally relaxed. With God on the inside and a totally new body I walked boldly to our coach and took my seat.

After a couple of days, we left the dessert region of the south where we stayed on the Kibbutz and drove to the lush green vegetation along the high mountains in the north to Galilee. It got better. I knew I was in the Holy Land but the surroundings began to look more and more like the land in which I was born and reared, Jamaica. There were acres of banana plantations, mango trees and all different kinds of trees. Melons and other fruit were being sold on the wayside, just like in Jamaica. The streets were cleaner and wider but everything else looked so much the same.

Throughout the journey the theme of standing and walking alone with God governed my life. It was absolutely incredible how different people came to associate and support me at different points and time. In recognising the pattern, I avoided holding on to anyone and just watched and accepted that God was at work in my life. I suddenly desperately needed the bathroom. I saw how God made the way to save me embarrassment. Only God could have made it possible. The coach stopped at a spot so that we could look over to Galilee, our next destination. It was absolutely breath-taking. The peace that engulfed me was unbelievable. It was preparation for what was about to happen. At this point I still shared with the same roommate though the relationship had become distant, but we were still civil to each other.

Whilst in Galilee one of the brothers had news that his father had died. I was honoured that he wanted me to be a part of his support network and to join in leading a prayer meeting. We met in one of the lady's rooms. We had a wonderful time in praising and giving God thanks. I returned to my room quite late. The night was still and the Galilean sea next to our base was calm, so was I. On walking into the apartment, I thought I had lost my way. There was a new person inside. Before I could apologise and make my exit she explained that she had exchanged places with my roommate because she was not happy sharing with me. No surprises. I saw something coming even though I was not sure in what form it would have manifested. I smiled, welcomed my new roommate and went to bed. Along the journey, God had made her one of my arms and I remembered saying to God, she is so knowledgeable about the things of God, I wish we had more concentrated time together. Here it was.

I woke up early the following morning. On tip toes I tried to sneak into the bathroom without disturbing her so that I could get dressed and go and pray on the bank overlooking the sea as the sun rose. I was really discrete because I did not want to disturb my new roommate. As I was about to creep out of the door, she spoke, 'Karlene can I come with you?' I smiled and responded, 'Of course.' I waited until she sorted herself. Together we left the apartment. It was quiet, still a little dark. I felt stimulated as fresh air filled my lungs. We walked across the beach, (more pebbles than sand) to a safe comfortable place on the bank of the Sea of Galilee where we sat to be greeted by the sunrise. It was spectacular. Both of us turned to our Bible, although the portion of scriptures were from different passages the message was the same, be ye separated and dependent on God. We shared our hearts giving God thanks for the opportunity to spend that special moment together. Then we prayed, followed by a period of leisure collecting pebbles and shells. Later in the day the first roommate came with hugs and kisses and apologised for the underhanded way in which things were done. I felt genuine warmth and I accepted her apology. Nevertheless, there was a deep wrenching pain in my gut. I cried inwardly and asked God why He was isolating me. I would be lying if I pretended it was easy to accept. Anyway, the Lord assured me that He was separating me unto Himself. At times it was hard to accept, but my life had been marked with all the positive things He had done and was doing in my life. I had to accept. The rest of the trip continued to prepare me for the work God had planted in me.

Chapter 33

Now I understand

The experience in Barbados and Israel prepared me to meet the unexpected in Jamaica. Two weeks after we returned from Israel I was in Jamaica. I felt alone and apprehensive. For the first time, going to Jamaica filled me with anxiety, even though I was going to travel with my son, Pianki. It was his first trip back since he left in 1998, four years earlier. Over the last four years I had experienced unexplained separation from close friends and brethren in Christ whom I loved and treasured. There was physical, social and emotional strain. Alone I could pretend that things would be right soon, but with Pianki around, how could I.

On the morning before we departed for the airport I knelt at my bedside to pray to God for journeying mercies and to avert any difficulties that might be in store. Unexpectedly I had a vision in which Overseer Howe appeared before me. She was the founder of the local church I visit when on the Island. The church was within walking distance of the accommodation we would be staying in. Overseer Howe had many churches across the island and a couple in America. There was always a really warm welcome from her when I attended. I would be invited to teach Sunday School, minister from the Bible and sometimes give a testimony. This gave me a sense of belonging. As a result, I had become a part of her fellowship, long before it became my refuge from feeling like an outcast from Pastor Key's church I had joined.

I was barely acquainted with the Overseer having only spoken to her once when she came to pray with me when I first moved into the house in May Pen. Now thoughts of her plagued my mind. I wondered what God was saying to me, I tried hard to focus on the image that was vivid in my head, hoping for a revelation, but it was unclear. The door bell rang and the taxi had arrived to take us to the airport. The trip to the airport seemed very quick. I guess the deep conversation with the driver, who was a family friend, had taken my mind from the earlier vision of Overseer Howe.

Pianki and I checked in with lots of time to spare, which passed painlessly before we were safely airborne. We had not long settled into our seat, Pianki sitting in the middle and I in the aisle seat, when we started to argue. In his usual fashion, he shut me out by putting on his headphones, closing his eyes and reclining in his chair. It made me nervous. I started to anticipate a disastrous time in Jamaica. I feared that once he connected with old friends I would be left alone in the house. I muttered, 'Oh God, will Pianki make life difficult for me in Jamaica?' The negative experiences of his time in Jamaica often overrode all the positives. He was feeling very sore and it made him extremely angry. I tried to position myself so that I could see his face. I wanted to work through some of the poisonous feelings he was harbouring inside before we landed in Jamaica. I struggled to get his attention. As I sat forward and twisted my body toward him hoping to make eye contact I could feel the stare of the lady across the aisle burning into the side of my face. I felt embarrassed. I tried to ignore her, but she kept looking at us, not so much at me, but trying to get a good look at Pianki's face. I had no choice but to look at her. She smiled, 'Hello, do I know that young man?' she asked.

'Pianki, Pianki,' I said, tugging at his clothes, but he just ignored me. It made me even more embarrassed. I wanted to disappear. But she seemed to have understood my feeling and helped me to relax. 'Leave him, young people are like that,' she said. I smiled back at her, she continued,' 'He looks like someone I have seen in Wolverhampton.'

'Wolverhampton' I echoed.

'Yes.' She said as I sat back into my seat and got comfortable giving her my full attention, 'You could have seen him. He is studying at the University of Wolverhampton and living with his grandparents.'

'Oh, so who are his grandparents?'

'Mr. and Mrs. Rickard,' I said. She laughed out loudly and looked deep into my eyes, 'Are you Karlene, the one that was sick and moved to Jamaica where you have set up a school for the church? With gaping lips, I stared back at her, absolutely lost for words. She went on, 'Your mom is my good friend, and she is always talking about you. She has bought all the materials and bedding for our house in Jamaica. My husband and I were members of the West Indies Association. We are good friends with Mr. and Mrs.

Rickard. Last year we returned to live in Jamaica. I went back to England on emergency, but my husband is at home.'

When she said her husband's name I remembered our family discussing what would be an appropriate bon voyage present for them, in fact I had a major input in the decision. As she talked I could vaguely recall seeing him at the West Indian Association meetings. Our dad was the chairperson. Sometimes I attended general meetings to give support. Whilst we were talking she got out some photographs of their home in Jamaica. One by one she passed them to me. I was mesmerized by the building. Some months ago, I had seen this unusually shaped building in a vision.

In the vision I had visited Jamaica with Pianki and he was accompanied by a woman much older than him. The woman resembled my friend Dee. We visited the very house in the photograph; it was pinned to a large rock which overhung a precipice. There was a small river meandering in the gully below. The path to the house was narrow and treacherous, you only had to slip and you would head straight into the gully. We negotiated our way singly along the path to the front of the house which was set on a platform. The front had a dome shaped shutter made of corrugated iron. As we stood before the shutter it started to unroll and the inside became visible. It was bright with white walls, large glass panels and glass tiles. The shutter stopped and I walked inside and faced the wall toward the back. It was a sheet of clear glass. The ceiling was low, adequate to accommodate my height. I could touch it, but as Pianki and his friend entered, the ceiling gradually rose until his six foot plus frame was standing comfortably upright. Pianki stood in the middle of the room, looked around, then faced me and said, 'This is not for me I am outa here.' No sooner had the words left his mouth than both he and his friend vanished. I looked to the left of the room. It extended into the woods almost becoming a part of the woodland. It was dark and scary. I could see the sky as the ceiling was also glass. I was alone. I pirouetted for a while, in a state of confusion. Then I heard a familiar voice coming from above, behind the rock on which the house was pinned. The voice was that of the founder and mother of the church I attended in England, Mother G, 'Karlene why have you built there? I am going to build in Mandeville.' There was no one in sight but her voice was loud and clear. I wanted to run, but felt trapped. I stood and pondered to myself. 'Why would Mother G want to build in Jamaica, after all she is from Barbados.' Then I moved into the next room. It illuminated as I crossed the threshold. The light inside the house followed me about.

I held the picture of the lady's house and stared. I had only seen that design in the vision, until this moment in the photograph. I could not believe my eyes. I had to share the vision with her. She listened carefully holding on to my every word.

'Amazing, you must come and visit us, you and Pianki. I have to tell Waldron when I get home. Let me give you the address.' I needed no encouragement to get the address. I wanted to see that house in its natural state. We talked for the rest of the journey. As the plane was near landing, Pianki stirred. I tugged at his clothes.

'What now, mommy?' he grunted. 'This lady has been trying to talk to you for ages, she knows you, and she is a good friend of your grandparents.' Immediately he put on a pleasant face, looked across to the lady, grinned at her and said, 'Hi.' I was angry with him. I thought he behaved disrespectfully toward me, I knew he had heard me calling him earlier. As my anger subsided and I reflected on the new experience, I was convinced that once again God had made a way for my time in Jamaica to be fulfilling.

The plane landed safely and smoothly. The passengers gathered their hand luggage to depart. I sat patiently and waited to be assisted by the air hostess, a part of the wheelchair service for disabled passengers. Sil, my new acquaintance left, promising to wait for us in the arrival lounge. There were many wheelchair passengers to the few wheelchair attendants. The process of getting through immigration was unusually slow. What used to be a fast track path became the slowest. When we eventually reached the arrival lounge most of the passengers including Sil had left. Mr. Key had come to meet us. He looked weary and frustrated. His wait had been extended by his early arrival to drop off a passenger for the plane on which we arrived. He grunted a welcome without his usual warm embrace.

'How comes you are the last one?' he asked. I could feel that he was annoyed. I managed to fumble a few words of apology, feeling guilty that I had him waiting for us, but there was little I could do. We shook hands as if we were strangers. He left us standing at the pick-up point whilst he went to get the car from the car park. It felt like the first time when Pianki and I came to Jamaica. He was only six years old then. The wait was not long, Mr. Key returned to load up the car. Pianki, gave me a look that said, 'This will not be a comfortable trip, all sixty plus miles.' My stomach churned and my heart started to race really fast. If I could have gotten back on the plane, I would not have hesitated. First Pianki and his attitude on the plane and now this. It felt as if I was in for a trying time in Jamaica. Pianki and I got into the car as Mr. Key put the luggage in the boot. Then he got in to the diver's seat without saying a word and we set off. A few minutes from the airport he spoke. 'We will be caught up with evening traffic and Mom will be wondering where we are.' It made me very nervous wondering who else I would be upsetting.

This was a journey which I always looked forward to; driving along the road in the middle of the sea, the fresh breeze on my face and the warmth of the heat permeating each cell and detoxifying my body and releasing me of the stress caused by living in the big city of London. I shared the news of everyone and everything like an excited child bursting to tell her parents. This time I loathed the thought of having to be engaged in a conversation with someone who I sensed did not want to know. My focus was on the long journey ahead, if only I could have shortened it. The journey on the road through the sea was more comfortable than I anticipated but at the end we joined traffic merging from all directions which was intensified because of the bumper to bumper rush hour traffic which Mr. Key had predicted and was trying to avoid. This brought our movement to a grinding halt. I tried desperately to think of the right thing to say, measuring ever word. Mr. Key's words were few. I hoped Pianki would have helped me out, but in his usual fashion he was fast asleep on the back seat. What I would have done to exchange places with him. The silence felt cold and hostile. My mind wandered to the many trips Mr. Key and I had made in the past, especially to the country - the laughter, the engaging conversation, the fun. He was like a special father, but now we were like strangers. It was painful.

I must have drifted in and out of sleep several times. Since I could not recall passing certain land marks, I realised we were nearing our destination. We were now travelling on the new stretch of motorway which gave us something to talk about. I was impressed at the marvellous job the engineers and builders had done. We flew along. Although it was dark, it was like being in the middle of a postcard, as the terrain was silhouetted by the towering street lights and the stars in the sky. I felt at peace with my environment.

Home at last! I was tired and just wanted to curl up in my bed and sleep. Pianki woke up, full of life, ready to explore. He helped Mr. Key to unload the luggage from the car and put them into the lounge. The placed smelled fresh of lemon polish, the glassy floor tiles sparkled under the light from the ceiling bulbs and wall lamps. Everywhere was squeaky clean. It was then I remembered I had forgotten to arrange to have the place cleaned but Pastor Key had obviously taken care of the situation. I really appreciated her kind thought. Had it not been so late and me being so tired I would have gone to say thanks. I decided to do it first thing next day. Pianki went off to see her, followed by Mr. Key. I stayed alone and flopped on to the settee ready to sleep. I was drifting into sleep when Pastor Key arrived, followed by Pianki. He had brought a small pot of food. Had he been alone I would have asked him to put the food away until the next day, but Pastor Key's tone and presence caused me to sit to attention. I took the pot from Pianki and started to help myself. I was very nervous. The atmosphere was fraught with tension. With every chew I waited for the explosion. Then she started, 'I had to miss a special graduation to supervise the cleaning of this place, you did not even ask me to do it'.

She went on and on. I wanted to cry why? Oh why? For many years I have been a part of the family, I gave of my best and initially I was accepted as a daughter. I didn't know what I had done so wrong to have tipped the pendulum of love in the opposite direction. Our relationship had gone sour. It had actually curdled. I reflected on the experience in Israel. God had prepared me for this time, it was hard to accept. The people who once showed me so much love and sensitivity were now quite distant. I recollected when I first arrived on the island in 1988 how one of the church members had greeted me with a beautiful mango as if she had picked it and saved it especially for me. Another had made me a beautiful pink dress. Now here I was alone, living in fear. Certainly, the theme that unfolded in Israel continued to be real. I needed to lean totally on God instead of depending on people. I knew that God was right because I had allowed the Keys to become my idols. For a long time God tried to alert my attention but I was dismissive of Him. The time had come for me to start to grow my own wings and fly with God as my only compass. It was not easy, but it had to be done.

Like a frightened child, I kept apologising to Mom for not being in touch and inconveniencing both her and her husband. My stomach kept churning over and over, my muscles tensed and water oozed from my pores. My clothing became saturated with perspiration. The terrifying experience must have been obvious to Pianki. When Pastor Key left he asked, 'Mom, you were frightened nuh true?' Submissively I muttered 'Yeess, son.'

At that moment I just wondered what else was in store for me. I had planned to visit Pastor Key the following day, but that was now the last both mom and dad were friendly and engaging; light hearted humour was exchanged, but I was wary. I had lost faith and trust in them which made me cautious. At last we arrived in the church yard. I stepped out of the car hoping everyone would rush me with hugs, embraces and kisses which was the practice whenever I returned from England. My worse fear was not unfounded. Most of them greeted me as if we were strangers. I longed for the warm embraces and constant attention, but it was not forthcoming. I walked into the church feeling down-trodden and went to the adult Sunday School class. Dad was the teacher.

After Sunday school I went to my usual seat (about four rows from the front near the doorway to the passage), for the main service. I sat alone on that bench. Pianki sat at the back with his friends. It was a special service incorporating the graduation ceremony for the children who were leaving the church's kindergarten to start their primary school education. They were making a significant transition, a rite of passage. A set of children had reached a significant milestone in their lives. I was excited. I had no prior knowledge of the occasion, but was delighted to be there. 'This was certainly God's timing,' I whispered. 'I could not have planned it better.'

I was not prepared for what was to follow. The MC for the occasion acknowledged all the contributors who had set up the school and impacted the lives of the children. I was not mentioned. I went unnoticed, not even the usual welcome to the service was afforded me. The children looked really beautiful and the keynote speaker was a young man, a member of the church, with whom I had worked and had seen grow and develop over the years. He spoke eloquently with confidence. I was proud of him. I looked around hoping to make eye contact with someone, to share a smile, but that wasn't to be the case. I bowed my head to hide my embarrassment. I fought back the tears and took deep breaths and then returned to the moment of the ceremony. Once re-focused on the children it was not too difficult to enjoy the contributions. It was a well organised ceremony.

I sat and looked at everyone being photographed. I screamed inside. 'God.' Suddenly I felt a strong presence next to me. It felt as if a powerful arm was thrown around my shoulders. I looked to the right, I looked to the left but there was no one there. It was clearly God's, supernatural presence. My cry had been answered. Immediately, I straightened up from the slumped, timid position. My crushed spirit was restored and I started to smile, applaud and looked around freely as far as my eyes could see. I even made eye contact with a few people. When young Steven was being presented with his certificate, the memories of his early days in the school both mom and dad were friendly and engaging; light hearted humour was exchanged, but I was wary. I had lost faith and trust in them which made me cautious. At last we arrived in the church yard. I stepped out of the car hoping everyone would rush me with hugs, embraces and kisses which was the practice whenever I returned from England. My worse fear was not unfounded. Most of them greeted me as if we were strangers. I longed for the warm embraces and constant attention, but it was not forthcoming. I walked into the church feeling down-trodden and went to the adult Sunday School class. Dad was the teacher.

After Sunday school I went to my usual seat (about four rows from the front near the doorway to the passage), for the main service. I sat alone on that bench. Pianki sat at the back with his friends. It was a special service incorporating the graduation ceremony for the children who were leaving the church's kindergarten to start their primary school education. They were making a significant transition, a rite of passage. A set of children had reached a significant milestone in their lives. I was excited. I had no prior knowledge of the occasion, but was delighted to be there. 'This was certainly God's timing,' I whispered. 'I could not have planned it better.'

I was not prepared for what was to follow. The MC for the occasion acknowledged all the contributors who had set up the school and impacted the lives of the children. I was not mentioned. I went unnoticed, not even the usual welcome to the service was afforded me. The children looked really beautiful and the keynote speaker was a young man, a member of the church, with whom I had worked and had seen grow and develop over the years. He spoke eloquently with confidence. I was proud of him. I looked around hoping to make eye contact with someone, to share a smile, but that wasn't to be the case. I bowed my head to hide my embarrassment. I fought back the tears and took deep breaths and then returned to the moment of the ceremony. Once re-focused on the children it was not too difficult to enjoy the contributions. It was a well organised ceremony.

I sat and looked at everyone being photographed. I screamed inside. 'God.' Suddenly I felt a strong presence next to me. It felt as if a powerful arm was thrown around my shoulders. I looked to the right, I looked to the left but there was no one there. It was clearly God's, supernatural presence. My cry had been answered. Immediately, I straightened up from the slumped, timid position. My crushed spirit was restored and I started to smile, applaud and looked around freely as far as my eyes could see. I even made eye contact with a few people. When young Steven was being presented with his certificate, the memories of his early days in the school came flooding back. When the first set of children moved to class one from the nursery, Steven was still in the nursery. One day he came to me and said, 'Auntie Karlene can I be in the big class?'

'Yes, Steven, you can.' I gave him a hug. He ran and joined the class. He was a model student who fitted in very well. After lunch he came back to me, 'Auntie Karlene, mi tired can mi go and sleep with the babies?'

'Yes Steven,' I said. He went and curled up with the babies. This pattern went on until Steven was ready to stay with the older ones for the whole day. I was so proud of him. His first rite of passage! Now he was ready for another rite of passage, to main school. Recently I heard that he has taken his SATs exams for high school and achieved a place in one of the prestigious high schools - another rite of passage. Quickly, I raised my hand toward heaven, 'Thank you God for allowing this once totally paralysed woman to contribute to the development of these young lives.'

At the end of the service I could not wait to congratulate the pastors for a well planned programme. God gave me the grace to take that step. The Holy Spirit abiding within empowered me with supernatural strength to overcome the humiliating experience. I was able to genuinely and sincerely praise the pastors for the service. It was then that I accepted that another chapter of my life had closed and a new one was about to begin.

Chapter 34

He cuts and heals

I woke up early Monday morning, wanting to attend Prayer meeting at the Key's home, but there was an inner presence hindering me. I struggled with the decision. Then I remembered the situation regarding the teaching post at Mica Teachers' Training College. Once I accepted that God did not want me to accept the job but simply trust him, everything worked out well. Having remembered, I accepted my current position. Then I was set free, with an inner peace. From that moment every door of opportunity flew open. I felt I was free from human obligations. I was convinced that God would provide the resources and the human support whenever they were needed. It was clear that I had to move on. The close relationship with the Keys had come to an end. It was no longer in keeping with the plan and purpose of God. I must admit that I had known this for sometime but letting go is always difficult. After all I am as vulnerable as the next human being, seeking solace and security within human relationships.

Although, I felt free I wanted Pianki to be there with me and for me, but I saw very little of him. He was still very angry about the way I was treated at the graduation ceremony. He lamented over all the years I had committed to working with those families at his expense. He was really angry.

Most nights I was alone in the house, but every morning at 5.00 a.m. the Lord woke me. I was programmed like a robot. I started prostrate in prayer, followed by hours of Bible reading. Then I wrote under the inspiration of the Holy Spirit until the flow stopped. I would then play a cassette at random. It was amazing - every message was by Pastor T, one of my ministers from Worldwide Mission Fellowship. She played a significant part in my spiritual growth and development and at the time had become a work colleague on family issues. Each message spoke directly into my spirit revealing aspects of the new chapter of my life. The titles were, 'Be courageous', 'Put on your Christian uniform' and 'Are you too nice to know?'

Mid-week Pianki and I visited my grand aunt who resided with one of her sons and his family in Kingston, the capital of the Jamaica, which is approximately sixty miles from our home. Once we were in town I took the opportunity to telephone my new acquaintance, Sil, whom I had met on the aeroplane. I spoke to her husband, Waldron. They were excited and pleased to hear from me. They invited us to their home. I accepted and they agreed to pick up Pianki and me the following day. They were going to take us for a tour around the area first. They arrived on time in their trouper. Pianki was not there. He had gone to the barbers with his cousin and intended to meet with his friends after. I could see the disappointment on Sil's face. As the three of us walked toward their trouper, I glanced at them and smiled. Immediately, our acquaintance on the aeroplane replayed in my mind. I muttered to myself, 'God knew how my relationship would change with the Keys and provided this couple as a cushion to soften the blow.' Waldron helped me into the trouper and we were on our way. We talked a lot. They were excited to be with me, like old friends, we had lots in common. It felt good. They drove around the community giving me a grand tour. The houses were magnificent, some pinned to the face of the cliffs. Eventually we arrived at their home which was not far from my cousin's. It was unusual. It could be distinguished from a long way off, just like the house in my dream. As I looked at the building I was sure that my breath stopped for a moment. I muttered to myself, 'Is this real?' It looked somewhat like a space object. We approached through electrically controlled gates. Waldron cruised down the drive. We were perched on an incline. He parked in front of the garage. We got out to be greeted by their watch dogs. Sil and Waldron were amazed that they didn't have to shield me from the dogs, they liked me. Apparently visitors are usually terrorised by them.

Their home was absolutely beautiful. It was tastefully furnished, with a touch of English "cottage-ness" fused with Jamaican culture. My host and hostess were just perfect. They showed me around. Then we relaxed on the veranda where I could take in a panoramic view of Kingston and savour the warmth and brightness of the sun mingled with the cool breeze. It felt as I anticipate heaven to be. Waldron and I enjoyed the ambiance whilst Sil prepared the lunch. It was not long before we were summoned to a well laid table, decked with a range of dishes. Sil had even prepared me a vegetarian dish using vegetables freshly reaped from their garden. She discovered on the plane that I am a vegetarian. My thoughts were, 'Friendship comes and goes like the wind, but God is always constant.' I believe God had availed Sil and Waldron to be my new supporters for a time and season. That was the first of many. I enjoyed their company and it was delightful to be able to share the Word of God with Mr. Waldron who was searching for a spiritual path. He now has a personal relationship with God and has been baptized and is deeply immersed in God's work.

Although I was moving on with what Christ had purposed for my life, there were times when I desired to be back with Pastor Key and the members. My experience is akin to that of the Israelite's journey. They were delivered from bondage in Egypt but they had Egypt in their hearts and wanted to return. At times the struggle to rekindle the link drained me physically and emotionally. Eventually I gave in and decided to visit the church again.

One day I phoned and made arrangements to be picked up on the Sunday by the Keys. The reception was cold, but I pretended that things were okay. I was relieved that I had taken the step and hoped to have had peace of mind. Unfortunately, this was not the case. However, my mind was preoccupied with having fellowship with the members in the church near my home. There were warring thoughts as if I had to visit that local church even though I had already arranged to visit their Overseer during the course of the week. I tried desperately to block the thoughts but it was overwhelming and eventually I collapsed on the sofa from sheer exhaustion. I muttered, which was now a habit, 'How could I not attend my church, they will think I am jealous because I was excluded from the graduation.' The graduation service had left Pianki wounded. He was distraught and embarrassed, in fact extremely angry. His friends and some of the parents kept asking why I was not actively involved. Some even laughed at him. The experience hardened his heart against the Keys and he decided not to ever visit again. I tried desperately to persuade him but he just ignored me. In fact, he kept away from me. This caused me to look at Pianki's behaviour seriously and realistically, removing all the artificial layers and being truthful to myself saying, 'If my first Sunday was an indication of how things have changed, how will things be if I continue to visit?' At that point I went into the bedroom where I clambered into bed dragging the blanket to cocoon my body. I was exhausted and hoped to fall into a deep sleep so that everything would fade away. Instead I was tormented and

I was blessed to be allowed in early, after which time was spent eating and socialising. I made my way back through the cliffs with the same gusto. I really saw God at work in my life.

The next day we had an equally challenging journey. We ascended to the great height called Mount Nebo, possibly to the spot where Moses (who led the Jewish people out of Egypt through the red sea and into the wilderness) stood and viewed the Promised Land. Unfortunately, Moses was not allowed to enter in because He displeased God when the people tried his patience. He lost his cool and acted contrary to God's instruction. I stood and faced the Promised Land, peering into the distance. It was a vast plain. I felt a churning in my stomach. I smiled to myself. I was excited and grateful that I was privileged to be looking at the Promised Land and within a few hours I would be walking the terrain.

As I stared in the distance there was that "voice" again, 'Ask Pastor to pray for you.' Immediately I scanned my surroundings to locate Pastor. He was a short distance away talking to two ladies. Without hesitation I went over to him and said, 'Pastor could you pray for me, please.' Amazingly, he took me back to where I stood initially, placed his hand on my head and prayed. It was a prayer of thanksgiving. He thanked God for my life and that the promises for me were being fulfilled and that I would enter the Promised Land. He thanked God for giving me the gift of counselling and teaching of families and asked that they would be perfectly developed. When he finished he noticed that two ladies with whom he was speaking earlier had drawn closer to us. He invited them to come and pray with me. Again he reinforced aspects of the previous prayer for me and then asked God to fulfil His promise for their lives.

Pastor finished praying and the ladies walked away. My whole being felt light as if I could have flown across the gulf that separated me from the Promised Land. I stood and looked in the distance; the area was veiled by a blanket of mist. I could no longer differentiate the land, but there was inner peace and a mighty presence as if a warm comforting arm was thrown around me. I knew God was within me and His presence was there. I was ready to make the journey. Slowly, counting my steps I walked toward the building where many of the brethren were viewing historical relics. I went into the building. It was cooler than outside and buzzing with activities. Various people passed by me pointing out things of interest, but I had a mindset to be in the Promised Land where the next phase of my life would become clear.

That night I had a good night's rest, woke up early the Sunday morning and prayed. I enjoyed the pace of things, there was no need to rush therefore I was calm. The church started an hour later than Pastor Key's and it was only ten minutes walk instead of an hour's drive; heavenly, what a blessing! I had enough time to spare; I relaxed in front of the TV and watched a televised church service - something I had always wanted to do.

When I thought it was near time for the service I walked to the church only to be faced by an empty building. It was quiet, I went and sat on the second row of the left side facing the rostrum, organised my bag and books, and then knelt down to pray. I raised my voice and thanked God for rescuing and giving me such a beautiful morning. Then I sat down on the bench again waiting for the others to arrive. By now church should have started, but it was still empty. Whilst waiting I reached for my Bible which flipped open to Psalms 11, my eyes went straight to verse 3 'If the foundation be destroyed, what can the righteous do'. I read it; stopped; thought about it; then kept reading it over and over. After, reading it several times, other related scriptures came into my mind. I turned to each one. As I read all the scriptures a message was being strung together like pieces of a jigsaw. I was so caught up with the process that I was unaware of the change in the church. By now many people had arrived and were scattered all over the building.

'Welcome Sister Colene' caused me to jump. I turned to see the young Evangelist Madden beaming at me with opened arms extended toward me. I stood up and we embraced. She held me tightly. Whilst saying, 'It is so good to have you with us again Sis Colene', she added 'I know God has given you a word for us today will you be the speaker for the morning service?'

I almost wanted to stay in her arms, to be saved from the role she had just placed on me. I knew I could not refuse because God had just given me the word.

After the evangelist there was a queue to greet me. One after the other including the three pastors hugged me. I felt loved and appreciated and very much at home. What was even more surprising was that the assistant Pastor, slid the Sunday school book into my hand and said, 'Now you are back you can take your job and teach the Sunday School.' She went to the rostrum and brought a chair which she placed in front of the pews.

After a brief period of singing and praying aloud everyone went to their Sunday school classes. The adults who included the two pastors and me sat together facing the empty chair. It was then that it dawned on me that I was the teacher so I whispered to one of the pastors, 'I thought you were joking.' We smiled at each other and I took my place in front of the class. Although the session was unplanned, it was powerful because everyone was engaged as we unpicked the lesson together. The content of the lesson spoke volumes to my heart. It was clear that the Lord was demanding my attention and wanted me to share with the congregation. After the morning service, Missionary Barnes invited me home for lunch, she lived across from the church, and there I learned that their Overseer had just returned home sick after her trip to America. That made my visit urgent and intentional.

Early Monday morning, I woke up, prayed and set out to visit their Overseer. When I arrived, her bed was already surrounded with visitors, but it was remarkable what happened as I entered her room. Her eyes focused on me. She greeted me. I could feel a lot of love coming from her. Suddenly she turned to her audience and started to esteem me as one being introduced to bring forth a message. I sat at the foot of her bed and started to massage her swollen leg whilst her visitors spoke. Although she was conversing with them, her eyes remained focused on me. I could feel a deep spiritual connection. One by one the visitors filed out of the bedroom. We were the only human beings left in the room but the presence of God was evident. Without any social interlude we started to discuss aspects from the Book of Job, she unfolded deep meanings of the scripture. I listened intently, it was both interesting and informative, but I really wanted to hear from God through her mouth. I knew she was a prophetess. I could remember when she visited our church with her team some years ago, how they prophesied over various people. Back then, I hoped I would receive a prophecy, but I was not included. Now I wanted mine. When I could wait no longer I interrupted her flow in exegesis of the scripture:

'Have you not got something to say to me from God?'

She laughed loudly with a little squeak like a mischievous child and said, 'Sister Karlene I have been waiting for a word from you'.

'Me Mom! I retorted, thinking how could she expect ordinary me to bring a Prophetess, a Word from God. I was not prepared for what came next, but then can I really say I am prepared for all the mysterious happenings in my life? My mouth opened and I looked deeply into her eyes and boldly declared, 'The word for the moment is Be Still!' She in turn started to pen the song 'Be Still', reading every line as she went along. Before I left she had completed a song entitled 'Be Still'? Every word she wrote was appropriate for my life's journey. 'Be still', became the theme for the yearly celebration kept in their church. When she finished, the "voice" spoke, 'Take Overseer through Job 38 and emphasize that I, God created all things for my purpose and you need to 'Be Still' and pen what I am saying to you. You cannot go back and redo what has already been done. It is done. Now is the time to pass the mantle to the next generation.'

I was besides myself. I spoke harshly with authority. We were together for hours, by now it was getting dark and I was both exhausted and hungry, but there was a settled peace inside, I knew I was obedient to God. I stood up and bade her goodbye. She wanted to feed me, but I was compelled to leave immediately. I left. Once in the taxi, I reflected on what went on in the room. Some of the Word I had spoken to the Overseer came back. It was then that I realised that I had spoken some strong words of rebuke. I felt as if I had over-stepped the mark by speaking with such presumption to an elder especially a mighty servant of God; a prominent person in the community, a founder of over twenty churches in Jamaica and others in America and a trainer and mentor to many pastors. But how could I really have understood what went on in the room? So, I just relaxed in the taxi and thought no more of the experience.

When I got home I hoped Pianki would be there, but the house was empty. It was so quiet, even the night beasts were asleep. I would have liked Pianki to be home. However, I was consoled by the thought that although we rarely saw each, whenever we got together the moments were revelatory and precious. God had given me a second chance to know my son. We got to know each other better than before. God had clearly engineered something special for us and showed me that He is the rock of my life and all I need is Him. Different people were being brought into my life and everyone demonstrated signs of being sent by God. The presence of God was constant and there was no need to make any demands on anyone. I just needed to rest on God.

Chapter 35

A friend from England

I was excited about the arrival of Doreen from the UK; she was coming to stay with me for two weeks. I had made all the necessary arrangements, but awaited confirmation of the flight so that I could ask Deacon Key to assist. I had not heard from her for a while but decided to call on the Keys to ask for help with my visitor. As soon I got into the Keys yard and greeted them, my mobile rang. It was Doreen. I was excited. 'Karlene I have arranged to be collected by my cousin.' I was relieved having been saved the embarrassment of asking a favour when I knew the door was closed.

On the day of her arrival I cooked, prepared her room and waited patiently. The flight was late. Hours passed, I got impatient. Quietly I prayed, asking God to make the way safe and clear. Soon after she rang 'We are caught up in bad traffic, so we are running late. Sorry I will not be able to stay very long with you because we have to get to my auntie's home in the country before it gets too dark.' When I heard that my heart sank. I was greatly disappointed. I thought Doreen was going to stay with me. I must have misunderstood her intention. When she arrived it was literary hi and bye. All that preparation! God was hammering home the message about not being dependent on others. He would only bring people, as and when I needed to be with them. It is never easy to accept being alone so much. I can echo the words of the five-year girl that said to God, 'I know you love me God but I would like a God with skin on.'

The following day, I recovered and was ready for anything. Within me there was a compulsion to visit my new friends in Kingston. I packed and left immediately. (On route I called my cousin to ascertain that it would be okay to spend sometime at his home. He sounded pleased as if he always wanted me to come and spend a long time with them). I was met at the bus station by my friend Pastor Loney. We spent the rest of the day together. It was fun. We shared, laughed, cried and prayed. He was a great source of inspiration, especially whilst I was ill in hospital. God used him to take me for hospital checks. Our visit was always prayerful. With him prayer is the basis to everything. Later that evening he took me to my family. As I pulled my luggage down the pathway to their home, I rejoiced in my heart, giving praise and thanks to God for making all the provisions and guiding my every step. The following day I was picked up again by my friends, Sil and Waldron. They took me to different places and introduced me to new people. My time with them was both reflective and relaxing.

During my stay in Kingston I met different people and shared with them, the parenting programme that God had placed in my heart. Every person I spent time with was right for that moment. Each time I opened my mouth I became increasingly confident about the work of parenting that I had to do. I started to develop a special, supernatural love for all those with whom I had become acquainted. I started to love again those who had hurt and rejected me; a forgiving spirit had taken over. Even the tramps along the road won a special place in my heart. I wanted to reach out to those who needed to be loved. I was ready to enter the world of hurting people especially children who were being abused. I even started to love myself more. A thought came into my mind which was partly scriptural, 'What can man do me but destroy the body, a body that fades anyway with time.'

It was at that point that the experience of standing on Mount Nebo in Jordan looking across to Israel to the Promised Land, Canaan, replayed in my mind. There we were at the possible spot where the prophet Moses who led the Israelites out of Egypt had stood and looked at the Promised Land yet was unable to enter. But I was privileged to do both with the blessing of my pastor. Pastor G placed his hand on my shoulder and prayed that as I entered into the Promised Land I would take up the mantle to counsel and teach many nations; bringing them into the knowledge of the love of God which would bring about healing for their families. I then remembered when his father had prayed for me in his living room before his death. He assured me that everything would be okay. Finally, I remembered the eve of being rejected by many in Jamaica, how a missionary had visited the church, (it was during our convention). He said, 'I have to do this before I sit down.' He placed his hand on me and said 'Children around the world will come to you for counselling. You will bring them love and joy. There will be laughter and they will be loved by you.' It made me feel positive because people around me were no longer very warm or friendly. I took time out to think about Moses. I was humbled by the experience, knowing that I made a journey that he was denied because the people he loved and served disturbed his spirit sufficiently to cause him to disobey God and to lose out on entering the Promised Land.

Everything was coming together, the experience in reading Jeremiah 1, then being rejected and so on. I marvelled at how God works. He allows people to come together and he separates them. Within each relationship His purpose for their lives is fulfilled. However, he gives us choice and if we decide to journey without Him there is usually mayhem and total disaster. On the other hand, if we walk with Him there are tremendous blessings, even though they are not without pain or uncertainty.

After a well-spent time in Kingston I returned to my home in May Pen and the opportunity came for me to visit Montego Bay for the first time. Doreen returned to spend sometime with me and we decided to visit her friend. We travelled on public transportation. The journey was long; at times it was nerve wracking as the young drivers sped along the narrow winding road with the mountain to the left and a sheer drop to the right. When I was not being nervous I was able to look at the absolutely breath-taking landscape. It was beautiful! Despite what seemed near-death experiences as the drivers manoeuvred the road, Doreen and I enjoyed our time together, laughing, joking and sharing childhood memories of Jamaica. As we progressed toward Montego Bay, there was a different feel to the environment. It felt fresh and light. The streets were clean. It reminded me of Galilee, the northern region of Israel. Calmness pervaded the place. We stopped at midpoint in Ochio Rios where we relaxed for a short period and ate some local dishes before going on to Montego Bay. I was not disappointed with the city. It was small but beautiful, clean, calm and the people were friendly. We took a local cab to our final destination. Doreen's friends were an elderly couple who had returned to live in Jamaica after living in England for a long time. They lived in a large beautiful house which was perched on a hill over-looking the town and giving a panoramic view of the city, the surrounding towns and sea. They were pleased to see Doreen and welcomed both of us. I felt as if I had known them for a long time. They were warm and friendly.

The following day after a hearty Jamaican breakfast of Ackee and salt fish the gentleman took us to tour the town. He pointed out historical and beauty spots, then left us on the beach near the main shopping centre. Hastily, like one parched for water, I got into my swimming costume and rushed out to the beach. I went near to the water's edge leaving Doreen at the entrance of the resort deciding what to do. I looked back and there she stood. I sat down and started splashing water over my leg. As far as my eyes could see there was a great expanse of blue water, it was calm; children were playing in it, adults floating and swimming and a there were a few boats in the distance. With the sun beating down on my back, it felt safe and comfortable so gradually I inched into the sea. There was a sense of freedom. As a non-swimmer I am normally very cautious, I respected the sea and usually was not in a hurry to take any chances, but not that day! I was lost in my own safe, beautiful world. When I came back to reality I had extended my arms shouting, 'Free at last, free at last' which resulted in me bumping into some white children and their mother way out in the depth of the sea. They were actually making way for me to pass and looked a little nervous. I don't who was more nervous at that point. My feet could not touch the bottom. God steered me toward the beach and I made a couple of frantic strokes which got me out of trouble. Had the family not been in the water who knows how far I would have drifted and what the end result would have been? I struggled to my feet, just about touching the bottom and waded to the shore where Doreen was now sitting next to my bag. 'You appear to be having such a wonderful time I could not resist the temptation.'

We stayed for a little while, and then made our way to the restaurant on the beach, some three hundred yards away. The place was creatively designed and there were tempting smells of tropical dishes. It was packed with tourists eating, drinking and just enjoying themselves. Once we purchased a small snack the only available place to sit, was towards the back which meant missing out on the full view of the sea. We sat at a table with a young black man; amazingly he was a Londoner visiting Jamaica for the first time. We talked about the goodness of God and he decided to accept Jesus Christ as his Saviour. I was excited by the new soul coming to the Lord and wanted to tell others. After finishing our snack, we bade him farewell and encouraged him to keep the faith and made our way to a boutique across the road from the restaurant. There was a friendly atmosphere there. Doreen was really bold and continued to talk about Jesus Christ; it gave me the confidence to do likewise. In between trying on some of their beautiful outfits two other people accepted Jesus as their Saviour. I hardly wanted to return to my home, but our time was rapidly passing. I bought a sarong and we left. It was certainly a challenge to get back to the elderly couples' home but we made it.

After a wonderful time in Montego Bay we returned home. Doreen stayed over-night. The following day when she was ready to leave I walked and stayed with her until she got a taxi then I continued to the Keys, just to say 'Hi'. It was the most harrowing experience I ever had. A simple 'Hi' turned into a seven-hour meeting. I was summoned to defend myself on several accounts, but I had developed such confidence that I was not prepared to take ownership for what I had not done. Whilst I was in the meeting my mobile rang. It was Doreen; she had travelled for miles to another town where she had been robbed. She was distressed, but so was I. I was unable to offer any support. She was surprised that I was still at the Keys and wanted details which I could not give so I abruptly terminated the conversation. I sat upright in what appeared to be a court room on the veranda, where I faced the judge, jury and witness in the form of two persons who I thought loved me very much. I quaked as I heard the accusations, rejection, and dismissal. The words cut deep into my heart. My legs became spasmic and my internal organs churned. Internally I threatened to leave, but I could not muster the energy to go. So I sat and listened, once again I felt when the Lord shielded me with His mighty presence. I heard the reports that were made by the brethren that I thought loved me. I did not believe what I was hearing so I wanted to hear from them directly but it was unlikely. I am sure I was guilty of some of what was said, but many things were out of context. It was impossible to unravel the details so I just listened, refusing to accept. I wanted to bawl but would not give the courtroom the benefit of seeing me weak and helpless. I was saved when an emergency brought the meeting to an abrupt end. The Keys were required to visit and pray for a sick relative in the local hospital. I was left sitting, too afraid to stand especially as I was unsure whether my legs would support me. Tentatively, I struggled to my feet and walked out to the path, heading for the gate when Pastor invited me into the car to be taken home. Obediently I went and sat on the back seat. It was a short drive to my home. In the past I would have been invited to visit with them in the hospital, but things had changed. I climbed out of the car and bade them good night and promised to pray for their relative.

The experience was difficult and uncomfortable but it prepared me to handle many hurdles. As I was about to enter my house I felt the Spirit of God directing me to my neighbour's house. It was after seven and it was very dark. The only light was a dim light in his bedroom. It seemed inappropriate to be visiting a single gentleman at that time of the night, but I obeyed. The gate creaked as I unhinged it and struggled to push it open. I quietly walked over to his bedroom window to attract his attention being careful not to be seen by anyone or to stumble on the rubble in his front yard. He said that the door was unlocked and invited me in. He was knee deep in Sunday school literature, Bibles and concordances preparing his Sunday school lesson. It was based on Proverbs 6. The section that resonated with me was verse 16, 'There are six things the Lord hates, seven that are detestable to him: haughty eyes, a lying tongue, hands that shed innocent blood, a heart that devises wicked schemes, feet that are quick to rush into evil, a false witness who pours out lies and a man who stirs up dissension among brothers.' We had a blessed time exegesing the text and making the lesson appropriate and interesting to meet the needs of the children. It ministered to me personally, unknown to my brother. When we finished I felt cleansed and freed.

As my neighbour walked me home I felt liberated and equipped to meet the next challenge in my life. At no point did I share where I was coming from or what had taken place. Although I have since told him of my experience and how God used that meeting to set me free me yet again! That night I slept like a baby. In the morning on reflection I knew the journey was not about the Keys, but God was moving me out of my comfort zone to re-establish my relationship with Him and to be prepared to fulfil the purpose for which I had been called. Soon I returned to England relieved to be away from what had become a hostile environment.

Chapter 36

The next stage

I was back in England, doing community work, attending church and happy to be away from the hostility that had become a part of my life. One day I was meeting with Robert, the cofounder of the Supplementary school, to discuss the future. Whilst we were planning, the Lord impressed on me that I should make a visit to Jamaica during the last week of May and the first week in June during which time I should visit my granddad and the local church which I often frequented. I told Robert who phoned his friend at the travel agency and the flight was booked immediately. Soon I was on my way. I arrived on the island the last Friday in May. The Saturday morning I chartered a car to visit my granddad. When I got to his newly built one-roomed house, perched on the hill where I once lived, I was overcome with emotion. I left the driver in the car and went under the bamboo parallel poles which stretched across the gateway into the small yard. It was a struggle to negotiate the large stones up the slight incline.

'Papa' I shouted. There was no response. I went up the incline to the back of his room and continued to the old house just above where he had built his room, and called again. The neighbour, Aunt Vie came out of her house. A wide grin of warmth spread across her face.

'Hello Mackie ah suh i good to see yu. Me nuh know where Mast Pa dey. Me hear im early dis morning so he shudn't be too far.' Then from the furrows in her brow I could tell that she was really trying to figure out where he could be. The silence was tangible and I broke it by saying, 'Thank you Aunt Vie' as I turned to go down the path. I hoped he was not too far away. I positioned myself on an escarpment so I could see our little plot of land in the distance and peered, but could not see any human figure. I walked back to the entrance of the building which was on the opposite side of the road. 'Hello' I shouted, 'Have you seen Papa'. The voice came back, 'You looking fih Mast Pa?'

'Yes,' I said. The woman came out into the open.

'No, perhaps im gone round Comfort to Mr Reggie ground to do sum wuk'

'Thank you,' I said and started to walk towards Comfort's. En route was the cemetery so I decided to visit my grandmother's grave at the same time. I knew that it would be a challenge, but I was determined. I had gone about a hundred yards when I saw a petite figure walking sprightly towards me with a bag in one hand and a machete in the other. I continued to walk toward him. He was moving at a rapid pace. As he got closer I recognized him. 'Papa', I said, still walking towards him. We embraced. His voice quaked as he repeated, 'Mackie, Mackie ah how yuh do. Me did tink dat me did hurt yuh and yuh mudda mek yunna nah write me. Last night me was reading de Bible yuh lef me and me wundered why yuh not bin in touch.' I placed my hand around his shoulder and we walked to the house. We talked and laughed about all sorts of things,

'Paps you should be visiting me, look how strong you are.' He laughed and said 'I will be 90 years in August and me never bin to see de doctor yet. One time me was going because me had gall stone and mi friend told mi sey, "No mast pa cut a piece of that toona" he pointed to the cacti type plant in the yard. 'mi boiled the toona and drink it. In no time mi pass out every gall stone. Then he looked at me seriously and said 'If anyone trouble dat plant a mi and dem.' Then his demeanour changed as he looked down into my face (he being at a higher point) as we were standing outside the house. His eyes were filled with tears, 'Mackie it was hard to tek yuh to de airport. Me wanted to stop time, and when we reach me wanted to grab yuh outa de car and run away wid yuh. Yuh was such a brave little girl. You never give up. One-day rain cum down and wash way every ting. The two goat stuck pun de cliff and nobady could get them. It was raining heavy and yuh disappear. How in God's name yu get them but wi see yu leading de goats'. There were tears in his eyes as he said 'you were always rescuing something.'

At that point my eyes were also filled with tears. With my childhood memories having been so sketchy it was really good to hear that I had done some good especially since things had turned sour with the Keys who made me sound like an ogre. I was really enjoying the childhood memories. I loved him intensely and I wanted to be reassured that he had a good relationship with God. He confirmed that he did and I returned to my home feeling satisfied because his life was right in Christ.

During that period in Jamaica, I was always alone in the house and one morning the "Voice" woke me and said, 'write.' That was the birthing of the A to Z of Parenting. He mapped out what should be included under each letter. It correlated with the parenting programme that He had previously given me. Many people had an input into making that programme culturally diverse and sensitive. When I returned to England and met with my friend who helped to edit the manual for the parenting programme, "Empowerment for parents". I shared the contents of the A to Z of parenting with her. She liked it and stated, 'So that is a part of the parenting programme.'

'No, I retorted as if it should have been obvious, it stands on its own' I said. Her response was:

'Well some of it will have to be rephrased'

'Okay, let's do it now.' Immediately we started to work on it. Over a period of time I would elicit thoughts from individuals- professionals, parents and young people, to shape the contents to make it inclusive and culturally sensitive, then I asked my friend to help with re-editing. The process went on for several months. I reached a point when I sensed that God wanted me to put the A to Z aside for a while and refocus on the Empowerment for Parents Parenting Programme. I had to trial it with parents from different racial and cultural backgrounds and to make appropriate changes to the programme in order to accommodate a range of parents irrespective of class, race, culture or gender.

In 2005 my friend recognized that I needed extra help with the parenting manual. Perhaps I was burdening her too much. Anyway, she called a meeting at her home with me and another friend to discuss how they could support me. It was a wonderful idea. Unfortunately, that was not the outcome. My friend wanted to establish a new company with a name she already had decided, the work of the company would be embracing a lot of my work. I was not happy but needed the help so I went along with the discussion and her plan. As we were working out the way forward I shared what I had done so far and the help I now needed. After speaking I played the wonderful promotional DVD produced by my son which outlined the structure of the programme. I could see that both my colleagues were impressed and excited, but my stomach churned because it suddenly dawned on me that in two weeks' time I needed to deliver Strand B of the programme to a group of parents in my church and the DVDs referred to in the programme were not yet made. The first one was about The British School System. I expressed my plight. Jennifer, my new friend smiled and said 'that is my area of specialism.' In my heart I thanked God and quietly said, 'You have done it again God' Then I turned to Jennifer and asked 'Would you be able to come to my church in West Norwood on Saturday and talk to the group of parents on The British School System and I will ask my son who is also my business partner to come and film it live. He can then edit it and produce a DVD that would be used in future programs'. I continued, 'I know it is many miles away from where you live and I can only cover your travelling expenses and lunch.' Without giving my request much thought Jennifer said, 'Yes as long as I am given clear directions.' Everything was agreed.

This started a revolutionary development to the Empowerment for Parenting Programme. I decided that for all the DVDs I would arrange for the relevant speakers to attend the sessions and be filmed while speaking to the participants and then this would be edited by Pianki to create the DVDs for the programme. I was absolutely grateful to God. Inwardly I kept saying 'Thank you God for the insight of using experts in action to develop the DVDs. What an awesome God you are.'

After the meeting I worked on the details for Strand B of the parenting programme identifying the experts to be invited for the different topics and making corrections according to advice. The first two on my list to be invited were Jackie who had worked extensively on the development of Strand A, (her area of expertise is Special Educational Needs) and my beloved friend Ankhara (who had also worked on Strand A) to cover Exclusion and so on. I reflected on the idea of having a presenter for the parenting group. I thought it would make the DVDs much more interesting and credible than if they were filmed in a studio. I looked at the topics and the dates when they would be needed to be delivered to the parenting group and prayed asking God that the experts would be available, then I contacted them and made my request. All of them were pleased to participate.

The journey to further develop the DVDs for Strand B had begun. For the programme to have developed I knew God's hand was on it. Even for the cover of the manual to be designed He had appointed a church brother Mike who is a professional graphic designer. He even used the photograph of his own family along with another family in the church and other parents that I had worked with from the Asian community. He was very patient and willingly made all the requested changes. He did not ask for payment and even apologized if he was late in completing any task. The end result was fantastic.

It was amazing how God spoke through so many people to work with me to produce such a powerful parenting programme. God birthed my second child "Empowerment For Parents" I am not sure if it took nine months to be formed. Pianki, worked extremely hard to produce all the DVDs that are an integral part of the programme. I was now at the point where I was ready to train facilitators to deliver the parenting programme to parents and carers. I had no idea how to proceed, but God had everything in control. Unexpectedly, my dear friend Ankhara who had all the essential skills, abilities and experience to make it happen suddenly wanted to join me in Jamaica from late December 2005 to mid-January 2006. I had tried for years to get her to visit me in Jamaica and she was not interested. Now she wanted to leave her family in sunny, beautiful Barbados over Christmas to come and spend two weeks with me in Jamaica. I had intended to visit Jamaica around that period but I had not yet booked my flight as the only available seat was too expensive. She was so determined to be with me in Jamaica over that period that she was even prepared to go ahead of me and wait for my arrival. I knew it had to be God. He had positioned her to help me to develop the training plan and to prepare me to train facilitators to work with parents and carers.

Amazingly, I managed to get a flight at a reasonable price and I arrived on the island a day before her. The flight was delayed, which meant that I arrived in Kingston late so I decided to stay overnight with the Loneys, my good friends who lived near the airport. This was convenient for me to collect Ankhara the next morning and for us to travel to my home in May Pen. Her flight was on schedule. It was exciting to meet her knowing that we were going to spend some time together exploring parts of Jamaica that I had dreamed about but never managed to visit. Before leaving England I booked for us to spend a period in Negril, situated at the western point in Jamaica, with miles and miles of white sandy beach. I arranged for a taxi to take us to exotic places. Unknown to me Ankhara had booked for us to have a special massage in St. Ann's at a treatment centre which was a part of the Jamaica Grand hotel complex, one of the most expensive hotels in Jamaica.

Along with all the programme materials that I packed, the Lord had prompted me to take the A to Z of parenting booklet to work on. When we arrived home Brother Stan had put everything in place and prepared well to make us both very comfortable. In the past he had made preparation for me, but not to this extent. In fact, he was a little disappointed when I had not arrived the previous night because he had cooked a special meal.

My time with Ankhara was certainly cathartic and empowering. A lot of emotional and physical healing took place for me. She introduced a medication and some natural remedies which proved to be invaluable to my physical health which in turn impacted on my mental and emotional state. When she left I was well prepared to train the first cohort of facilitators.

During our time in the little apartment on the beach in Negril I woke up at six every morning to pray followed by one hour working on the A to Z for parenting before going for a long walk along the beach. It was the best holiday I ever had. Once my friend left I relaxed, visited friends as well as my granddad and also appeared on a national television programme.

I returned to England toward the end of January and started the training immediately, contrary to the advice of Ankhara but God wanted me to start. I have learnt that it is important to know the voice of God and that when He speaks the advice of experts can be overridden. The training was a resounding success even though some things needed to be changed. That training session gave me insight and experience to develop the programme further. I enjoyed it and scheduled other training sessions. I was just gathering momentum in the training when He spoke, 'Put down the parenting programme and focus on the A to Z of parenting.' I got my friend who normally does my first stage of editing before using a professional editor to correct what I had written. She made some corrections. I then passed it to a copy editor, she too was familiar with my style of writing and raised some pertinent questions which caused me to rethink and re-examine the contents of the book. Once I had made some changes I passed it to ten individuals in the field of parenting which included teachers, parents, therapists and parenting experts. Everyone had something useful to add to the book. I was okay with how it had evolved and was ready to publish within God's timing. He had even provided the illustrator, a young woman called Earla. Initially I intended to use my relative in Florida, who was only ten years old, to illustrate. She had produced some excellent pieces which had impressed me. Then I realised it was not practical with the distance between us so I approached Brother Mike with regards to taking some appropriate photographs. I showed him my relative's illustrations. He thought that illustrations would be better than photographs so he told me to approach Sarah, a young lady in the church. He suggested that she could do the initial work and then he would improve on them.

One day I phoned who I thought was Sarah and asked her to meet me in the back hall after church to discuss the work. She agreed. After Sunday school I sat at the table waiting for her. Sarah came through the door accompanied by another young lady. They both moved towards me. Then Sarah turned and left the room while the other young lady advanced towards me. I thought it was strange. Anyway she came and introduced her self, 'I am Earla, we spoke on the phone. I am at University doing illustrations.' I was shocked. The only time I had heard that name was when the youth leader was allocating names to different people for prayer and I was given her name. I prayed for her for several years but we had never met. Now she was about to illustrate my book. When I fed back to Brother Mike and showed him a sample of her work he too was surprised. He never knew she could illustrate. Again God had worked on my behalf by putting Earla in place.

The training of facilitators to deliver the parenting programme that God had given me had started well and I was enjoying it. There was still a lot be done but God was saying that I should focus on completing the A to Z for parents for publication. My friend who edited my work was not happy because she felt I was being hasty and the standard would be compromised. This challenged our long-standing relationship because I was insistent that God had instructed me and it would be done. To avoid any acrimony, I withdrew from looking to her for help and said to God, 'You say Lord I must publish this book I need the help to do it'. He sent that help and the book became a reality.

I was compelled to show Pastor G the final version before it went to the printers 'Karlene,' he said 'the bait is wrong, change the cover make it more inclusive. It is a book for everyone.' I went back to Brother Mike. To be honest I thought he would be angry, but he graciously redesigned the book to meet the dead-line. I gave little thought as to the amount to be printed as God had laid on my heart 10,000 copies. Then my son said, 'You cannot produce less than 10,000'.
Unexpectedly Doreen who was now involved with the book also said, 'You must print 10,000'. I had no choice but to print 10,000. Many people said you are a brave woman, why have you printed so many. Others said that they will not be sold.

Chapter 37

He is constant – the same today as yesterday

God continues to speak even louder than before and what He said at the beginning, He reinforces and brings to pass. In August 2006 after I returned from having a break in Rome I went to church. It was the graduation service for the parenting group. Rev. T and I had not met before Rome to plan and I had forgotten that it was the graduating service. I was going to go home after morning service, but now I couldn't so Mother G invited me to have dinner with her and Rev. T and to go over the programme and prepare the introductory speech. We sat down at a well spread table to part take of the meal prepared by Mother G.

Rev. T shared about the wonderful time they had away on retreat whilst I was in Rome, then she said, I was asked to speak from Isaiah chapter 54 at a convention on the Saturday after we returned, and I could not think what to say, but God took over. Immediately my ears were on stalks because she was talking about the scripture that God has given me over and over. I wanted to hear every word. Instead of explaining how God took over she took off her jacket and left the table in a hurry to return with her Bible and then she started to minister to me. Eating stopped. She stared in my eyes and these words flowed like a stream from her mouth. 'Don't be afraid, do what the Lord called you to do, stretch out your tent cover over a large area. Don't limit God, just stretch out the Tent. The Holy Spirit will secure those tent pegs et cetera' she went on.

At first it was scary, hardly what you expect at dinner especially when you are hungry and enjoying the meal. Anyway after she finished there was a warm flow through my body. I looked beyond where she sat and I remember when her Dad stood in that spot and spoke over my life. Before I got carried away with the memory Mother G took over and starting to pray for me. I could see that much life had left Rev.T and she seemed tired. When the ministering was over, we had not finished our meal and it was time for church. Rev. T and I still had not discussed the programme and I certainly did not prepare a speech.

The service was unusual in that this was the first graduation service not addressed by Rev. T. She asked Rev. G to do it. When it was my turn to speak, the Holy Spirit filled my mouth. I was confident and comfortable. There was an anointing upon my body. It was the start of a different chapter in my life. From that Sunday I found that I ate, drank, and breathed about parenting everywhere and there was always an audience of people wanting to know more.

Despite the growth in my spiritual life and the intimacy with God and the doors that were being opened (I made a presentation at the International Federation of Parenting which impacted on many lives) I continued to struggle with personal and family issues. There was still a feeling of rejection and sometimes questioning of everything I had accomplished through Christ.

I decided to visit my parents. I had not seen them for a long time and my Dad was not keeping in good health. The drive was long and tiring, but I arrived safely. As I pulled into the driveway my youngest sister pulled up along the kerb simultaneously. I went into the house leaving the door open for her. It felt good to be at home and to see my parents. They were watching TV. I kissed them both, and they seemed pleased to see me. I sat waiting for my sister to come but she never did. Instead she went into the kitchen. When I felt rested I went into the kitchen. Unexpectedly she was angry and started to pick an argument with me. Many issues surfaced and she provoked me to anger which made me confused. I went back into the living room. I had come to appreciate that God was working in and through me and it was time to visit some family issues with my parents. I did. It was both cathartic and revelatory. I recognized that the devil wants to put a block to my healing and consequently hinder me from working with broken families. I try to remain calm and composed throughout the process.

My mother had a partially erroneous impression of the life I lived as a child in Jamaica. She thought that unlike when she was growing up, I had experienced a grand and privileged life with my grandparents and that I had been spoilt. She talked about being there for me as a child; which puzzled me at first considering that I had only met her when I was twelve years old. On reflection I remembered her letters and gifts and the fact that she wanted me to join her at a younger age. She was also able to express her feelings about my ex-husband and the reason why she thought I became ill. She remains very angry at him for assaulting me.

I shared some of my supernatural experiences. Each time my mom finished my story because they were also true for her, it was then she started to appreciate that we had a similar journey. Strangely it reminded me of how I tend to take over when my son is sharing his hardship stories with me. One day he said 'Mom why do you always want to take away my difficult experiences.' A necessary door had been opened for me and a lot of healing took place. I could sense that my mom was still hurting.

I read what I had written about being abused to her. This made it easier for us to talk. However, for a moment my relationship with God created a stumbling block. My composure while reading gave her the impression that I was hiding behind the cloak of God and displaying perfection without human frailties while judging others. It was an opportunity to bring clarity and to express my daily challenges and how God enables me to face them. My mom became overwhelmed and left the room but dad, and I continued to talk, (like the old days when we used to garden, decorate the house, manage various community projects and attend meetings). He shared his experience of growing up in Jamaica. It was really interesting learning about his childhood and adolescent experience. His mother was a significant part of his life and he drew strength from her. She was full of wisdom and had a clear focus on fairness. I sensed that she was particularly protective of Dad because of his kind and caring nature.

This conversation prompted me to tell my son how much I love him and share the experience I had with my parents and how liberating it felt. When I phoned him I did not handle the situation well because I got side tracked with another issue which made him angry. I tried to calm him but we parted on a very uncomfortable note. The next day he was abrupt and rude to me on the phone and I hung up on him as I was not prepared to be spoken to in that manner. He phoned back and apologized. This drew us closer together. On return to London our relationship continued to be strengthened.

The time spent with my parents provided lots of healing for me. I was able to reflect on my childhood experience and let go of the past. Since joining them I sometimes felt rejected not being comfortable with my accent and my identity. I had lost a sense of who I was and was living in the shadow of my sister who is nearly just over a year younger. I was able to put everything into context and understand my mother's pain and journey in part. I was now ready to accept and love myself. There was no longer any need for a facade. I was freed.

Chapter 38

The future

Some time had elapsed since my friend and I were at variance over the A to Z. We met and resolved our differences. She gave me a book - Healing Toxic Emotions. She had ordered a different book but this one had arrived instead and she decided that it was for me. It was not a book I had ever heard of or thought I needed, but it was relevant to every area of my life and I found it difficult to put down once I started to read it. From that experience I accepted that many people will come and go out of my life. Everyone has a special purpose maybe for my growth or to pass on something that I need to deliver to someone else. Whatever the purpose, I need to accept that they are passing through but that my communication with God needs to be constant.

In January 2007 I felt that God wanted me to train up someone who could train facilitators to deliver the Parenting Programme, so that I could be released to minister to families and carers on parenting issues in different parts of the world. Although welcoming the opportunity, I became nervous and possessive of the programme. To me handing it over was another loss, like losing a child. I felt heavy. I phoned my friend to share what I thought God was saying to me.

It is clear that the Parenting Programme and the A to Z of Parenting were indeed a part of my journey. They are tools that can be used to heal hurting parents of their shame, fear, anger and guilt and prepare them to embrace their emotions and use them positively. God has told me that millions of the A to Z of parenting will be sold.

I have developed a love for working with the media and public speaking on family healing, and parenting issues. It is time for me to minister about family values, relationships and emotional literacy in churches and in schools. I also have a vision to purchase a building to establish a family centre for hurting women in Jamaica.

Throughout the year God has continued to close and open chapters in my life. In October 2007 the "voice" instructed me to leave World Wide Mission Fellowship. To my surprise I was ordained as a Minister of the Gospel in December 2007 while in Jamaica.

'God has opened a new door for you, go through. The way has been made. You are pregnant and you must give birth.' Those words, uttered by an unexpected visitor while she prayed for me at my home in London, arrested my attention. I could not plead ignorance because God had already spoken to me. South Africa, China, and Australia are some of the places where He will send me. I plan to share my story to help people to find comfort and more importantly, salvation in Christ Jesus. Earlier in the year during a break in Hawaii I saw the awesomeness of God. Fear, love and respect gripped me causing me to release more and more of my will to Him. I have accepted my purpose and I am both excited and apprehensive about the future.

God has made me into a parenting guru. I have written the acclaimed PMEC parenting manuals and He has given me the mandate to work with parents and train facilitators. This has taken me from the UK, round the world and back to Jamaica.

God has made into a parent guru I was appointed as parenting specialist under the Archbishop of Canterbury in the UK for the Christian and Moslem alliance, at each meeting young Moslem girls sat at my feet calling me mother and asking me for teaching I got nervous and resigned, I felt God was angry with me, so I requested to be reinstated, they laughed and said it was not possible. When I thought God had given up on me, I decided to spend most of my time in Jamaica, I became a member of the Duhaney Park New Testament Church. Unexpectedly I was appointed, for a year, as the Parenting Director.

Fast forward to 2021, and I am on the board for Parenting Places a one stop shop parenting initiative rolled out across the island of Jamaica in 2020. I have written the acclaimed PMEC parenting manuals and been mandated to work with parents' facilitators, this is taking me around the world. In 2021 I have co-authored a pocket book entitled, "What makes Children Fly" with a fifteen years old flyer currently attending Campion high school in Kingston Jamaica.

www.ingramcontent.com/pod-product-compliance
Lightning Source LLC
Chambersburg PA
CBHW061218070526
44584CB00029B/3886